MODESTE MOUSSORGSKY

Portrait of Moussorgsky by Ilya Repin

MODESTE
MOUSSORGSKY

by Victor Seroff

Funk & Wagnalls NEW YORK

TO JOAN KENNEDY

Look not on her to despise her,
Turn not away from her so.
They are more blessed and wiser
Who can forgive, for they know.

—"THE OUTCAST," A SONG BY MOUSSORGSKY

MODESTE MOUSSORGSKY

❧ *One* ❧

MODESTE MOUSSORGSKY was born into a family whose ancestors could be traced back through thirty-two generations to the Rurik, the first Russian dynasty (862). But he was neither a prince nor a count, for by the fifteenth century Modeste Moussorgsky's branch of the family had lost its princely title and had become country squires who, with only a few exceptions, preferred administering their large estates to military or civil service in the government.

Modeste's father, Pyotr Moussorgsky was the illegitimate son of Alexei Moussorgsky, an officer in the Preobrazhensky Guards, and Irina Yegorova, a pretty young serf. Alexei eventually married Irina, and their son was legitimized. Pyotr served eight years in the Senate (1814–1822), and then he retired to settle down on one of the family estates near the village of Karevo in the Tropez district of Pskov province. In 1832 he married Yulia Chirikova, the daughter of a landowner in moderate circumstances.

They had two sons, but both boys died at the age of two:

Alexei I (1833–1835) and Alexei II (1835–1837). Despondent because of these misfortunes, Yulia insisted that an additional first name be given to her third son, born in 1836. She was prompted to do this by a century old Russian custom, a custom based on the superstition that "since evil-wishing people could harm a person through witchcraft," the best protection for a man is to disguise his identity by an extra secular name.*

Thus, although Yulia's third son's baptismal name was Evgeni, he was known by his secular name—Philarète.

Apparently, three years later, that is, a year after Philarète had survived his first two fateful years, Yulia felt no need to give an extra name to her fourth son—Modeste. For some undisclosed reason Modeste Moussorgsky had always insisted on March 16, 1839, as the date of his birth, though actually he was born on March 9.

Traditionally in those "nests of gentlefolk" a boy's childhood passed under the supervision of nurses and governesses. Children in their infancy were closer to their nyanyas than to their parents. Their intimacy with their nyanyas was shown even in their way of addressing them, which was in the familiar, while with their parents they used the more formal mode. In his childhood Modeste's nyanya was

---

* The baptismal name of Czar Ivan III (1440–1500) was Timofey, and Boris Godunov's (1551–1605) was Yakov. A baptismal name was usually known only to the man himself, his parents, and his godfather, and remained secret until it was disclosed at his burial service. This custom began to disappear in the eighteenth century, but remained among the peasants even as late as the beginning of the twentieth century (Nikolay I. Kostomarov, a well-known Russian historian, in his article "Family lives and customs among the Great Russians in the Sixteenth and Seventeenth Centuries" published in 1860).

his constant companion and his playmate. She wove her
fairy tales based on the legends that particularly abound in
the Pskov province, one of the oldest provinces in Russia.
Some of the tales were terrifying and kept the boy awake at
night, for her descriptions of witches and demons and their
evil spells were so vivid that Modeste imagined that the old
manor house in which he was born, with its surrounding
dark forest, and Lake Zhizhitza, with its fearsome reputation, were inhabited by gnomes, giants, and all manner of
weird and mysterious creatures. These stories, in addition
to developing in the sensitive boy an extraordinary gift of
fantasy, left indelible impressions on Modeste and were, he
said later, the main source of inspiration of his musical im-
provisations, long before he had learned the elementary
rules of piano playing.

Modeste was more attached to his mother, for in this
class of Russian society children did not become close to
their fathers until they were fully grown. Yulia was one of
those romantic natures, born and bred on a landowner's estate in a remote province of Russia so admirably portrayed
in Russian literature. The rare visit of a neighbor was their
contact with the rest of the world, an event to be long remembered, discussed, and sometimes given an importance
out of all proportion. For it could have meant the realization
of a young woman's cherished dream of falling in love with
a man who would marry her and introduce her to a glamorous and adventurous life.

Otherwise, their youth was spent with the female members of the family and their governesses, from whom they
learned French and German, singing and playing the
piano. Or they passed their days in solitude, reading ro-

mantic novels and poetry in the shaded alleys of a garden; and so they were inevitably led to daydreaming and writing their own poetry, sometimes even in a foreign language, claiming that their own was not adequate enough for the expression of their delicate feelings.

One of such poems written in Russian can serve as an example of Yulia's endeavors in poetry.*

Twenty years had passed
Since we had met.
At that time he was
An officer in vogue,
He was handsome and well built
And how often his fiery glance
Had turned the heads of young women!
I was young and innocent,
I fell immediately in love with him.
I was young and beautiful,
And like his, the glance of my eyes
Knew how to conquer young men.
I loved him, and he loved me,
And our love led our flirting to
Where everything was joy.

. . .

Twenty years had passed.
Suddenly we met again;
At his brother's I found
My lost officer.
Oh Lord! What a change in him!
It was my sister-in-law
Who had to tell me his name.
Overcome by sorrow
I hastened to return home. . . .

* From the French translation of the original in Michel R. Hofmann, *La Vie de Moussorgsky* (Paris: Editions du Sud, 1964).

There, upon my entrance
My husband and my children
Comforted me
With their love. . . .

The "pastoral" charm of these young ladies seemed to
have been their *raison d'être*. Their education was limited;
no demands were made upon them to participate in any
practical part of the administration of their estates—they
were reared solely for marriage and family. Yulia was an
exemplary mother—gentle and endowed with remarkable
self-control, qualities that influenced Modeste's character.
"She was a saint," Moussorgsky invariably remarked later
whenever he spoke of her.

Yulia fared better in music than in poetry. She taught
the boys to play the piano, but Modeste must have been one
of those children who are "born pianists," for it was due not
to her amateurish instruction but to his own talent that at
the age of seven he could play some of Liszt's less techni-
cally demanding compositions and, two years later, could
give a worthy performance of John Field's concerto before
a large number of guests at the Moussorgsky home.

Yulia was not alone in encouraging Modeste's interest in
music. His father was a great lover of music and played the
piano, although merely for his own pleasure. Both he and
Yulia should be credited with the discovery of Modeste's
talent and for having sufficient interest in giving it a chance
to develop further, rather than letting it remain as just another pleasant pastime.

Therefore, when at the age of ten Modeste entered the
secondary school of SS. Peter and Paul in St. Petersburg,
his father engaged Anton Herke to give Modeste piano les-

sons. The thirty-seven-year-old Herke had studied under a number of prominent pianists, including Kalkbrenner, Moscheles, Field, and Henselt, and he was popular in St. Petersburg as both performer and teacher. He was just what Modeste needed, providing a more disciplined and methodical training than that given him by his *maman*. But despite Herke's prediction that Modeste would develop into a great piano virtuoso, the Moussorgskys' enthusiasm could not stand in the way of the traditional choice for a Moussorgsky's profession, and that meant that he would have to go into military service—specifically the Preobrazhensky Guards.

For the first time Modeste had playmates of his own age, for while living at their country home his sole companion had been Philarète, but the three-year difference in their ages seemed to have had great influence on their interests. Almost nothing is known about the two brothers' relationship during their childhood, and just as little is known about Modeste's playmates at the secondary school of SS. Peter and Paul, until three years later, when he was sent to the Cadet School of the Guards, a preparatory school for the Preobrazhensky Regiment. There he found himself among boys of much tougher fiber and of different background and upbringing.

On their estates the Moussorgskys owned an "unknown quantity" of serfs (meaning a very large rather than a small number), and in his sheltered life in Karevo, Modeste probably was not aware that their relationship to their masters was that of slaves. He soon learned in the Cadet School the power of superior over subordinate as it was practiced among the cadets.

The students were mostly from aristocratic or wealthy families, and each boy had his own serf to serve as his valet. Should the serf fail in his duties, which included keeping his master entertained, he was punished and even flogged at the order of the school authorities. Each senior cadet also exercised his power over "his" junior cadet, who had to obey his orders to perform various "services," mostly humiliating, including being carried to the washroom on the younger cadet's shoulders.

To give distinction to their position, the senior cadets called themselves "cornets" and the younger students "vandals," and to be a "real cornet" was in the eyes of the school authorities the height of achievement. The students were not overburdened with scholastic studies for they disdained all homework, a disdain that was regarded benevolently by the school director, General Sutgov, who did not approve of his students doing "much thinking." They were eventually to become the "golden youth," whose main interest lay in wine, women, and song.

General Sutgov was particularly displeased with a student who drank common vodka. Nothing could gain his esteem as much as the sight of a cornet drunk on champagne returning to the school sprawled in an open carriage drawn by his own pure-bred trotters. It is obvious that Modeste was not suited to the role of either cornet or vandal, and that inspired by his musical studies under Herke and his own reading of German philosophers, he could only provoke the general into exclaiming, "What kind of an officer, *mon cher*, are you going to be?"

If Modeste survived this preparatory school and reached an officer's life in the Preobrazhensky Regiment, it was because of his capacity for pounding out mazurkas, polkas, and waltzes on the piano for his comrades' night-long dancing. This "service" somehow mellowed their haughty behavior toward one who did not participate in their horseplay. And because occasionally Modeste was asked (or was he ordered?) to play piano duets with the general's daughter at their home—a great honor—a certain prestige called for some respect from his fellow students.

His serious attitude toward his studies also played no small part in his resistance to the general system of the school. He excelled in history and literature, and thanks to his governesses, he had a perfect command of German and French. But above all, his interest in music, far from having been obstructed by the atmosphere of his surroundings, led him not merely to improvise while entertaining his schoolmates but to make his first attempts at composing. Since he did not have the vaguest idea of even the most elementary rules of composition, he had to be helped by Herke with his first piece—"Cadets Polka"—which Herke arranged for publication. Modeste's father paid for his son's debut as a composer.

At the time of his father's death in 1853, Modeste did not yet plan to abandon a military career in order to devote himself entirely to music. After four years at the Cadet School he was graduated with the rank of lieutenant and admitted into the Preobrazhensky Regiment. Now that the "cornets" had grown a little older, had become officers, their preparatory "training" for the life expected of the "golden youth" was to find fulfillment in the more exaggerated behavior of *bon vivants*—in squandering fortunes on parties, gambling, and drinking, but above all in striving to secure their futures by courting rich countesses or, at worst, rich merchants' daughters. In this respect Modeste's interest did not conform to the pursuits of other officers, and his limited allowance simply did not provide sufficient funds for frequent debaucheries.

Still, Modeste could not help acquiring the veneer of a Preobrazhensky officer: "polished manners," practice in dancing and attending the ladies, and an affected speech sprinkled with short remarks in French that would have sounded just as well in Russian. He also learned not only to drink occasionally, but now and then to participate in the officers' all-night drunken sprees.

Otherwise, despite his youth, he already knew how to behave on a given occasion. Thus, when not in the company of his comrades, the slight, well-groomed Modeste made a favorable impression. Dressed in a close-fitting uniform and holding on to his saber, which looked as if it were too big for his medium size, he was reminiscent of the pretty picture of a boy dressed for a masquerade ball. Neither the dreamy expression of his large grayish-blue eyes, nor his babyish mouth, nor his walking on his toes in his high boots, strutting like a rooster, could betray the crack regiment's reputation among the Russian forces.

He would introduce himself by offering his small hand with its carefully manicured nails, slightly bowing his head with its pomaded dark hair. Barely opening his mouth and with a blasé air, he would quietly pronounce his name, Modeste Moussorgsky, omitting the *g* and stressing the first syllable of his surname—it sounded more exotic to him. In fact, until 1861 he even signed his name "Moussorsky."

In contrast to the other officers, whose conversation ran the usual gamut of social gossip, races, and receptions, and the recitation of their amorous conquests, Modeste gently and thoughtfully discussed literature, the arts, and, of course, music, which was always on his mind. "*Je voudrais tellement être un grand compositeur*," he said to those who presumably understood French. He was going to write an opera, he said, and had already chosen his subject for it, based on Victor Hugo's romance *Han d'Ilande*.

He was usually asked to play the piano, a request to which he gracefully acquiesced, and he played and sang in his low, almost baritone voice excerpts from the two operas he knew, *La Traviata* and *Il Trovatore*, coquettishly throwing up his hands from the keyboard, while his enthusiastic listeners encircled him, sighing, "*charmant*" and "*délicieux*." The ladies smiled at him.

Modeste had been completely ignorant of Russian music until Feodor Vanlyansky, one of his friends in the Preobrazhensky Regiment, spoke to him about Alexander Dargomizhsky, and eventually introduced him to the composer. In the history of Russian music Dargomizhsky's name stands next to that of Mikhail Glinka: these two composers had laid the foundation of Russian National Music. Like the Glinkas, the Dargomizhskys belonged to upper-class Russian society. But although they were also of the landed gentry, they were not as well off as the Moussorgskys, and were members of the civilian rather than the military branch of the government service. Actually, it was only in their youth that both Glinka and Dargomizhsky held positions in the civil service; these, minor and more nominal than active, they resigned in order to devote themselves to music, since their incomes, derived from their families' estates, made them financially independent.

There is no record of Moussorgsky's first meeting with Dargomizhsky, but most probably it took place after the performance of Dargomizhsky's opera *Russalka* (*The Mermaid*) at the Maryinsky Theater in St. Petersburg in May 1856. Like Glinka, who, after the failure of his two operas, *A Life for the Tsar* and *Russlan and Ludmilla*, had left Russia in utter disgust (he died soon afterward in Berlin in 1857), Dargomizhsky, discouraged by the adverse criticism of his two operas, *Esmeralda* and *Russalka*, gave up any further attempts at public performances of his works and turned to "musicales," which he held twice a week at his home. "Here," he said as he welcomed Modeste, "meet all who love art, who are not bound by a career, some little position in the government, or the government's opinion—in fact, all the independent musicians in St. Petersburg."

Dargomizhsky was a little over five feet tall with a disproportionally large head; he was forty-four years old, but because of a sallow complexion that gave him a sickly look he appeared older than his age. Otherwise there was nothing striking about his outward aspect, even though he liked to wear a sky-blue jacket and a bright red waistcoat. He had a slightly turned-up nose, high cheekbones, small full lips, and a small thin mustache. But he did have an amazingly squeaky voice, which arrested the attention of everyone who met him for the first time. The surprising quality of that voice was the result of some complications following the measles he had had at the age of eighteen, and which affected his lungs. He would have had a pleasant tenor voice, instead of a *tenorino* or *falsetto*, had it not been marred by sounds that could have been produced only by a child. And yet this affliction did not stand in the way of Dargomizhsky's impressive delivery of his vocal compositions, which formed the bulk of his works.

Modeste soon learned that Dargomizhsky's musicales differed from those in society salons which were of a purely entertaining character in an improvised style. Since among Dargomizhsky's guests there were not many professional singers, he took as great pains in preparing the programs for each occasion as if they were being offered at public performances. With the male singers he worked every day at his home; but to coach the women, he was willing to go anywhere for, as he repeatedly said, "If there were no female singers, it wouldn't be worthwhile to compose." He liked women—indeed, most of his songs were written for the female voice—and he prided himself that "in the whole of St. Petersburg" there was not a single famous or talented female singer who neither was his pupil nor did not profit by his advice.

For the first time Modeste had met a professional musician—different from Herke, who was interested only in piano literature—and he was also impressed by the accomplishments of Dargomizhsky's pupils. They sang Glinka's and Dargomizhsky's compositions, for the works of Italian composers were either excluded or, if performed at all, served only as objects for ridicule. "We perform Russian music simply, without any sort of affectation," Dargomizhsky explained to Modeste. "In fact, we perform it the way our friend Glinka would like it performed. . . . I am not fooling myself," he added. "Most of our music lovers and press scribblers don't find inspiration in me. In their routine interests they expect only sweet little melodies. I have no desire to lower music for their entertainment. . . . I want music to express the spoken word. . . . I want truth in music."

Modeste knew next to nothing about Glinka or what he had tried to achieve in his operas, so scornfully rejected as music for illiterate muzhiks—"*C'est la musique des cochers*," in the opinion of the aristocratic St. Petersburg audiences. And Modeste knew nothing about Dargomizhsky's bitter disappointment, after some twenty years of struggling, at being considered merely as an amateur; as for Dargomizhsky's credo for his work, it was entirely over his head. Modeste had occasionally heard people talk about truth in literature, in painting, in sculpture, but this was the first time he had heard about truth in music. He could understand that in other branches of art it meant "realism," but "truth in music," "truth in sound," "to find a way of expressing the spoken word in musical sounds"—this was bewildering to him, and it would take Modeste some time before he realized Dargomizhsky's main ambition.

The word "truth" has a double-meaning in Russian: "verity," but also "justice." And when Glinka and Dargomizhsky, and later Moussorgsky, used that term in relation to music, they meant what today would be ascribed to "realism in music."

Modeste was young and eager to learn, and he became a frequent visitor at Dargomizhsky's Mondays and Thursdays. But he was shy and felt conspicuous in his elegant

Preobrazhensky uniform among the predominantly civilian guests, and so he was glad to meet another officer, an officer in the army engineer corps, César Cui.

Cui was of medium height, and while his delicate features were well concealed by a carefully trimmed beard and whiskers, and his gray eyes were behind eyeglasses, they failed to make him look older than he was—twenty-two, three years older than Modeste. Also, he gave an impression of being cold, which he was not. On the contrary, as Modeste soon learned, Cui was capable of a warm relationship, even an intimate friendship, but at first he was put off by Modeste's uniform—which proclaimed a membership in the "golden youth" with its none too flattering reputation—and thus he adopted an attitude not merely prejudiced but actually condescending toward Moussorgsky, the aspiring musician. Nevertheless, in a short time the two "comrades in arms" became best friends, and Modeste learned the reason for César Cui's foreign names and his background.

Antoine Cui, César's father, was a Frenchman who, during Napoleon's retreat from Moscow in 1812, was wounded at Smolensk, and like many other soldiers in the Grande Armée was left behind half frozen. Apparently the oath that Alexander I took at the beginning of the war with Napoleon—"We shall not lay down our arms until the last Frenchman has left Russian soil"—specifically excepted Antoine Cui. He had settled in Vilna first as a tutor to the children of wealthy families and later as a teacher of French in the Vilna *gymnasium*. He had married a Lithuanian by whom he had four children, and although his occupations were cultural and peaceful he undoubtedly had retained his admiration for military glamour, for he named his three sons after historical heroes: Alexander, Napoleon, and Caesar.

There was not much opportunity for a musical education in the small provincial town of Vilna—in fact, young César was lucky to have had some instruction from the Polish composer Stanislas Moniuszko, best known to us for his opera *Halka*. But after six months of study with Moniuszko, César joined his two brothers in St. Petersburg, and while Alexander and Napoleon were studying architecture and painting at the Academy of Arts, César entered the Military Academy.

Like Modeste, he was graduated with the rank of lieutenant, but his service in the engineer corps left him more free time for music than Modeste's duties in the Preobrazhensky Guards left him. When Modeste tried to play piano duets with Cui and discovered that he was not equipped for his part, César told him that except for the piano lessons he had received from his sister when he was ten, nobody had ever taught him to play the piano. And he admitted that he was not very interested in it anyway, since his sole desire, ever since he had known Moniuszko, had been to compose. It gave him a superior feeling toward Modeste, who so far had not had a single lesson in composition. But he liked Modeste, tried to help him to understand the constructions of composition; he spoke of Mili Balakirev, under whom he was studying, and suggested that Modeste do the same.

Moussorgsky's meeting with Balakirev, then a rising star on the musical horizon for whom Glinka had predicted a great future, was the turning point in his life.

❧ *Two* ❧

IN Mili Balakirev, merely two years older than himself,
Modeste met a fully matured man of exceptionally
strong-willed personality and wide erudition. Both
characteristics resulted from Balakirev's background and
the life he had led in the pursuit of his interest in music,
first in Nizhni-Novgorod, where he was born in 1837, and
later in St. Petersburg, where at eighteen he settled down.

Having neither title nor land, Mili's father earned
enough money by holding on to a minor government post at
Nizhni-Novgorod to support his wife and four children. But
Mili's mother, who had discovered her son's unusual apti-
tude for music, taught him to play the piano, and even took
him to Moscow for a few lessons with Alexander Dubuque,* who had gained a wide reputation as a teacher.
Lack of funds for continuing their stay away from home,
however, and the absence of any good music teachers in
provincial Nizhni-Novgorod would have left Mili's talent
neglected had it not been that Alexander Ulibishev, a pas-

---

* He was a pupil of John Field, who originated the nocturne—
that form of composition made so popular by Chopin.

sionate music lover, took the boy under his wing and provided him with the opportunities he deserved.

Alexander Ulibishev's remarkable personality was formed by his background and his unusual intellectual development in his youth. He was the son of a Russian Ambassador to Saxony, and was born in Dresden in 1784. Having received his formal education in Germany, at the age of sixteen he went to Russia, where, after completing his studies in St. Petersburg, he joined the diplomatic corps and served in various posts in Germany. Although he lived most of the time abroad, he had belonged (since 1819) to a revolutionary secret society—The Green Lamp—which had progressive political views and had fostered the unsuccessful Decembrist coup in 1825.

Ulibishev had been offered an ambassadorial post in Persia, but in 1825 he resigned from the Ministry of Foreign Affairs, and settled on his estate, Lukino, some thirty miles from Nizhni-Novgorod. In his retirement he did not emulate his neighbors, wealthy landowners, whose lives were passed in leisure, in supervising the management of their estates between the hours devoted to recuperating from gluttonous repasts and planning elaborate dinners for the following day, or in gossiping over cards at the Noblemen's Club in Nizhni-Novgorod. His independent means allowed him frequent visits to the capital to keep abreast of the latest developments in art, literature, and music. He was known for his translation of Dante's *Divine Comedy* into Russian.

And in Nizhni-Novgorod, Ulibishev at forty-one, with rosy cheeks, neatly framed by a thin gray beard, dressed in a loose tweed jacket and gray trousers, was a conspicuous figure in the audience of the local theater. There, once a week, he sat alone in the second row, apart from his wife and two sons who occupied a loge, and, as if he were a drama critic, he intently watched the performance through his gold-rimmed glasses. And indeed his reactions, which he vociferously expressed, were decisive for the fate of the play and the reputation of the actors, since the provincial audience closely followed his positive and negative gestures. It was known that when pleased with a performance, Ulibishev would pay as much as ten times the price of his own ticket and his family's loge. Still, music was his most absorbing interest.

Neither a musician nor a writer nor a Frenchman, he wrote in French a biography of Mozart. He began his work while still a bachelor, believing he could accomplish his task in a few months, but more than a decade passed before, as a man with a large family, he had completed the biography, which had grown into three volumes. (It was eventually published in French in 1843, and later translated into German and Russian.)

While this work evoked considerable interest among European musicians, it had, although indirectly, a far greater importance in the development of Russian music. Having soon realized how unprepared he was for his venture, Ulibishev had not only amassed a large collection of literature and musical scores, but had also organized a small private orchestra at his home in Lukino. He invited some of his neighbors who played various instruments for their pleasure to join him in this enterprise, and he selected the most musically endowed among his serfs. And to make this ensemble into a working orchestra, capable of acquainting him with the music he felt it imperative to know for his biography, he engaged Karl Eizrikh, the young Viennese conductor of the orchestra at the Nizhni-Novgorod theater.

It was Karl Eizrikh who introduced the twelve-year-old Mili to Ulibishev, and soon Ulibishev's home became the "school" that Mili so urgently needed.

Mili not only had access to Ulibishev's library and profited from his guidance and analytical discussions of the works, but by assisting at the orchestral rehearsals, he became familiar with, among others, such works as Mozart's Requiem, and Symphony in G minor, Handel's *Messiah*, and the overtures to *Don Giovanni* and *The Magic Flute*— to name only a few in the repertory given at Ulibishev's. And Mili must have observed Eizrikh's direction of the orchestra very intently, for two years later, when Eizrikh left Nizhni-Novgorod to return to Vienna, Mili, at the age of fourteen, took baton in hand and became a conductor.

Although Mili would have liked to make music his profession, he was not financially as fortunate as Glinka or Dargomizhsky, and so he had to prepare himself for a more practical way of earning his living. At sixteen he entered the univeristy at Kazan to study mathematics and physics, returning to Ulibishev's estate and to music only during his vacations. But Ulibishev felt that his protégé's talent should not be sidetracked, and after Mili had spent two years at the university, Ulibishev persuaded him to give up his studies and move to St. Petersburg. Ulibishev was convinced that with his assistance in musical circles Mili would make his way there as a musician. He introduced Mili to Glinka, who was impressed by one of Mili's first compositions, a Fantasie on themes from Glinka's opera *A Life for the Tsar*, written in a Lisztian style. Mili also proved himself a brilliant pianist. Although he later said, "If I can play the piano at all it is due entirely to the ten lessons I had with Dubuque," he also admitted that from the age of eight he never abandoned the piano, but played everything he happened to hear.

With Glinka's endorsement of his talent and Ulibishev's social connections Mili was able to obtain a sufficient number of pupils to be able to remain in St. Petersburg after Ulibishev had returned to his estate. He also played the first movement of his recently composed piano concerto at one of the concerts at the university on February 12, 1856, which brought his name to the attention of the music critics. But Mili was not interested in becoming a concert pianist, and he told Modeste that he could not care less about improving Cui's piano technique, for he was only interested in composition.

Actually, Mili was not equipped to teach composition. Not having had any proper schooling in harmony or counterpoint and orchestration, Mili firmly believed in acquiring this knowledge from experience; therefore, the "lessons" that he started to give Modeste in the middle of December 1857 were more of a music-appreciation nature. While playing with Modeste the four-hand arrangements of Beethoven's symphonies and various works of Schubert, Schumann, Glinka, and others, Mili explained to him the different forms of compositions.

Modeste was too timid to show Mili his own first attempts at composition—the "Cadets' Polka" (1852) and Souvenir d'enfance (October 16, 1857)—but Mili, without any fur-

ther ado, just told Modeste to compose a scherzo for orchestra and a piano sonata, though Modeste scarcely knew the
difference between the two. This left Modeste more helpless
than ever, for he admired Mili and would have liked to
please him with his work, but he simply did not know how
to progress once he had begun. Months passed. Mili was
still expecting to see Modeste's completed work, but all his
pupil could say was that he was working and was not yet
ready to submit his compositions to Mili's criticism.

Also, their lessons were irregular, because of Modeste's
duties at the regiment and sometimes simply because of his
participation in extracurricular activities with the officers
which left his mind less clear than it should have been. Mili
grew impatient with him, showed an obvious preference for
working with the methodical Cui, and would have given
Modeste up as unworthy of his attention had he not believed in his candor and his sincere desire to become a composer. Instead of their "irregular lessons," Mili preferred to
meet occasionally for what he called "a friendly exchange of
opinions." He would visit Modeste and his mother at their
home, and since Yulia took a great interest in everything
concerning her favorite son, Mili, when not at the piano,
tried to explain to them his newest ideas:

Symphony must no longer be constructed in four parts as Haydn
and Mozart conceived it a hundred years ago. Why *should*
there be four parts? Why should that never change? The time
has come for that system to pass into oblivion, as well as the
symmetrical and parallel construction within each movement.
We have done away with all the academic forms—odes,
speeches, and arias—in dramatic expression. Now the time has
come to forget about the first and second themes and the ex-
position—the *Mittelsatz*—in symphonic music.

"The analytic attitude often stifles the creative spontane-
ity," Balakirev said, and quoted Glinka: "The strict German counterpoint is not always good for the free imagination." He valued above all the strength of a thought: "The
picture created by a poet must contain an idea that should
point to a definite direction in life."

While sharing innumerable cups of tea with them, Mili
would talk, and Modeste hung on every word of the new
friend he had proudly presented to his mother. Yet he had
to admit to himself that he could follow only with difficulty
Mili's theories and plans for the future of a Russian music
not based on the established rules of European composition.
Modeste also discovered, however, that these were not Balakirev's own original ideas, but that he too had been introduced to them by somebody with a far wider *Weltanschau-
ung*—and that this somebody was Vladimir Stassov.

Vladimir Stassov, thirteen years older than Mili, was one
of the most distinguished figures in the culture of Russia in
the nineteenth century. He was intimately connected with
all the branches of the arts for almost three quarters of a
century. He had written innumerable reviews and articles
that had stirred wide and heated polemics—the most important among them on the works of Shakespeare, Lessing,
Tolstoy, and Gorky. (He was a close friend of both Tolstoy
and Gorky.)

The son of a famous Russian architect, he was born in
St. Petersburg in 1824. He acquired his first interest in
music through his friendship with Alexander Serov during
their school years (1836–1843) at the School of Jurisprudence. The two classmates were practically inseparable,
playing duets and attending concerts and the opera, but

while Serov had already chosen his profession of musician, Stassov's various interests kept him from deciding his future. Eventually, Serov became a composer and one of the leading musical critics, whereas for Stassov music was only one branch of the arts, and thus too narrow for him to devote himself to completely. The erstwhile close friends eventually drifted apart.

Stassov had spent several years in France, Germany, and Italy, hearing their music, visiting their museums, and in general enjoying his youth, until he suddenly realized that at the age of twenty-five he was "*zu alt um nur zu spielen, zu yung um ohne Wunsch zu sein.*" He passionately loved music—the years of his study of music during his friendship with Serov were not spent in vain—but he had no talent for composing, and he knew it.

Upon his return to Russia, he began working at the St. Petersburg Public Library (1850), and pure chance decided his career as a writer. When Mili Balakirev met him, Stassov was doing research work and ghost-writing for Baron Korf, Director of the Library. Czar Alexander II had asked Korf to write a series of historical articles, and the Baron in turn asked Stassov to "help" him. Thereupon, Stassov was "officially attached" to Korf's office, receiving rank and a high salary.

In less than seven years he was promoted to a civil-service status equal to that of a general, his salary allowing him to occupy himself with anything he was interested in, and from 1872 he was in complete charge of the arts department in the library. As for the decorations due him for his "help" to Baron Korf—these he did not begrudge the Baron's keeping for himself.

Stassov lived with his family, four brothers and a sister,
the wife of his brother Nicholas and their three daughters,
two aunts, and an adopted girl with her governess. They all
lived in the same house, which was open to their friends,
the cream of the intelligentsia, a new class in Russian society. Their home was the center of advanced liberal ideas,
influenced by the works of Diderot, Lessing, Chernyshevsky, and Alexander Herzen.

Having recognized Mili's potential qualities, Stassov
took great pains in "educating" him, for in Stassov's opinion
he was still only a provincial lad, not yet ready to join in
these discussions. Stassov spent many evenings reading
aloud to Mili, not only from Homer and Shakespeare, but
also from the works of Gogol, Nekrassov, and Pushkin, explaining their relationship to the history of Russia and to
the rise of nationalism since Napoleon's invasion of 1812.
He argued that music should also have its own national
character, that it was high time for the Russians to stop
borrowing ideas from abroad or imitating the Germans and
Italians, and high time for them to compose their own music
without any foreign accent. He realized that it was a difficult task, but he believed that Mili could become a leader of
such a national cultural movement and that others would
follow him. And Mili, in turn, already thought, although
purely intuitively, that Cui and Modeste as well could eventually be enrolled into Stassov's project. And so he passed
Stassov's ideas on to them, and also read with Modeste the
works suggested by Stassov.

The mass of new impressions and the demands of these
unfamiliar subjects on his concentration overwhelmed
Modeste. In a little over six months, a comparatively short

time, he had entered the musical circles that were simmering with activity. It was one thing to live among men who wore the same uniform, who looked more or less alike, and whose ways of thinking and behaving conformed to their position in the military service; it was quite another to find oneself among men whose personalities, life-styles, and relationships were entirely individual. Modeste was extremely sensitive to these first impressions.

The atmosphere at Dargomizhsky's musicales and the composer's personality were as new and strange to a Preobrazhensky officer as Dargomizhsky's theories were to a neophyte musician.

In Cui, Modeste had found a young man whose character as an officer was as different as their respective uniforms. Far from displaying the characteristics of a "golden youth," Cui was modest and completely satisfied with his lot, even though he was poor. "I think," he told Modeste, "I would be happy even in hell." In all his twenty-two years he had never been drunk; nor had he assuaged his youthful passions with loose women. He was in love with Dargomizhsky's pupil, Malvina Bamberg, a daughter of Rafail Bamberg, a druggist in Vilna, Cui's home town. In language that surprised Modeste, who was used to his fellow-officers' bravado in their descriptions of amorous conquests, Cui confided to Modeste his feelings toward Malvina almost reverentially. He spoke of their first kiss and of the exact moment when he had proposed to her, and he explained the nature of his first composition—a symphonic scherzo based on a combination of the letters B, A, E, G from Malvina's last name and his own initials, C, C.

Modeste was no less impressed, though entirely differ-

ently, by Mili, whose last name suggested a Tartar origin.
Mili was short and heavy-set; his practically square head
gave the impression of sitting directly on his shoulders, and
his short-cropped black hair and slanting, squinting gray
eyes completed an appearance of Mongolian character. Modeste was a susceptible young man, and what he heard
seemed to affect him as much as what he saw. To add to the
kaleidoscopic impressions, he was now introduced by Mili
to Stassov, who had a large beard and whiskers—giving
a patriarchical appearance that Modeste recognized from
the old paintings he had seen in museums. Stassov's basso
voice suited both his imposing figure and his manner of
speech: he expressed himself in loud *bach* (*bachnut* in
Russian means to slam down), and his friends had nicknamed him "Bach," but not in reference to the composer.

Through Mili, Modeste also learned about *Narodnichestvo*, as it later came to be known, a cultural movement
initiated by the intelligentsia, who directed their members
to "go to the people" and share their knowledge with them.
The Stassovs were vigorous champions of *Narodnichestvo*,
which was also part of a social movement that advocated
the freedom of serfs. It was not a simple matter for Modeste
to understand because of his close association with the men
of his regiment. Their roots lay deep in the feudal system;
sworn to uphold the absolute monarchy, they were still
adamantly against social reforms. It was difficult for Modeste to understand Stassov's theories and their relationship
to the creation of a national music—a Russian people's
music. "To the general public music was an acquaintance,
as it were," Stassov maintained, "with whom one shook

hands while passing on the street, and not a friend with whom one shared one's life. Literature, painting, and sculpture had already become a part of the national wealth, already marched side by side, and music must be made to take its place along with them." But what was clear to Modeste was that if music meant to him what he felt it did, he would have to choose between a military and a musical career.

And while so far, except for his passionate interest in music, there was not the slightest evidence that Modeste had the ability to become a composer, nevertheless, against the advice of his friends, Modeste Moussorgsky resigned from the Preobrazhensky Regiment on July 5, 1858, less than a year after he had been introduced to Dargomizhsky. He insisted that he had an excellent excuse: he was to be transferred into a sharpshooter battalion and within a year would have to move from St. Petersburg, thus leaving his family and recently acquired musical friends. He preferred to free himself from any service, and to go to Tikhvin in Novgorod Province for a cure, which his health needed urgently before he could begin the work of a musician.

And indeed it was imperative for him to attend to his health. The years at the Cadet School and later even his minimal participation in the officers' life had taken a considerable toll of his nervous system. He drank too much for the good of his frail constitution. The country air and a good deal of rest would restore him, he believed. But he soon began to miss his friends: with Cui entirely absorbed in his marriage to Malvina, with being completely out of touch with Dargomizhsky's circle, and with Stassov's disapproval of his resigning his commission, Mili seemed to be the only one on whom Modeste could depend for help and guidance in a new life, the life of an artist.

From the very beginning Modeste was aware of Mili's intellectual superiority as well as his strong-willed character. In their discussions Modeste, although sometimes irritated, had to concede to Mili's clearly and firmly expressed views. But Modeste's pride was hurt and his self-esteem incited him to stubbornness.

It led him to analyze others as well as himself and to discover his own failings. He believed that in Mili he had found an "echo" of his own thoughts, and he even reached the conclusion, although it was erroneous, that Mili's personality was akin to his own. He wrote Mili long letters, laying himself bare before him as it were, and giving him a detailed account of his mental and physical state.

October 18, 1859

Mili,

Our argument today was of such great interest that on my way to bed I determined to write you about this dispute— If Moses himself told the people "an eye for an eye, a tooth for a tooth," then I agree with you, because his is the fundamental law for the spirit and the policy of the people. It seems to me that this rule occurred to the people themselves independently of Moses, a consequence of harsh customs. —Your arguments— damnation and circumcision—are not enough: Christ replaced circumcision with baptism, which is somewhat gentler, but in essence is just as strange a rite. Damnation was prescribed for a crime, that is, for not carrying out one or another law; in place of damnation Christ introduced the idea of eternal torment—it is actually the same thing except that He softened it a little through penitence. This is my explanation; give me your written answer, in case you know for certain that it ["an eye for an eye, a tooth for a tooth"] was laid down by Moses himself.

On the following day, Modeste wrote to Mili:

You reproach me with two peculiarities that you assume to be present in me. I will begin with the first—mysticism—or, as you rightly express it, the mystic strain in my nature. Two years ago, as you know, I was in the grip of a terrible illness, which attacked me with extraordinary violence while I was staying in the country. This mysticism, aggravated by cynical thoughts about the Deity, became much worse after I came to Petersburg. I managed to conceal it from you, but you must have noticed its effects upon my music. I suffered greatly and became fearfully sensitive, even morbidly so. Then—either as the result of distractions or thanks to the fact that I gave myself up to fantastic reveries, which held me captive for a long time —my mysticism began gradually to disappear, and when my reason had gained the upper hand, I took steps to get rid of it altogether. I have made a great effort of late to conquer the thing, and fortunately I have succeeded. At present I have put mysticism far from me—I hope forever, since it is incompatible with a healthy intellectual and moral development.

On February 10, he wrote again:

Dear Mili,

Thank God, it looks as though I were beginning to recover from severe, unendurably excruciating sufferings, mental and physical— Remember how, two years ago, we were walking down Sadovaya Street together—you were going home—it was summer time. We had just been reading [Byron's] "Manfred." I was so wildly excited by the sufferings of that lofty spirit that I cried out: "How I wish I were Manfred!" I was a mere child at the time, remember! Fate thought fit, apparently, to grant my wish—I became Manfred for the time, literally—my spirit slew my flesh! Now I must have recourse to every kind of antidote. Dearest Mili, I know you are fond of me—then for God's sake keep a tight rein on me when we are talking together, and don't let me kick over the traces! For the time being, also, I must give up all my musical activities and avoid every kind of work that taxes the brain if I am to get better. My rule must be: "Everything must be done for the physical cure, even at the expense of the intellectual development." The reasons for my nervous excitability are clear to me now. It was not only the consequence of onanism (this is almost a secondary reason). The chief causes are as follows: youth, an immoderate capacity for enthusiasm, a strong, unconquerable desire for omniscience, exaggerated introspection, and an idealism that goes so far as to take the dream for reality. I see now that, at the age of twenty, the physical side of me is not sufficiently developed to keep pace with my forced intellectual growth. The latter got the upper hand and stifled the former. (Here is the reason for underdevelopment—onanism.) We must now come to its assistance; distractions—get as much rest as possible—gymnastics, cold baths, these must be my salvation.

Today Philarète and I have been to the ballet, a very charming ballet with many beautiful scenes. But the music, Mili, the music was terrible! The ballet made a strange impression on me—I was very nearly ill in the theater. When I got home and went to bed, I was at once assailed by extremely tormenting dreams, by hallucinations so sweet, yet terrible, so intoxicating, that to die in such a state would have seemed an easy thing. That, fortunately, was the end of my sufferings; I now feel much better—at any rate I am perfectly calm. . . . Mili, I feel as if I had awakened from a heavy dream.

He was reading Johann Kaspar Lavater's *Aussichten in die Ewigkeit* (1775), which was about the fate of the soul after death. "A very interesting subject," he wrote Mili. "As you know, I was always driven to the fantastic. Here is what Lavater says: 'The soul of the deceased transmits its thoughts to a man who is capable of clairvoyance and is informing him of its [the soul's] locality.' " He was also reading popular books on geology, and informed Mili that he had discovered that "Berlin was built on ground of infusorial earth, some of which is still alive!"

And as if to assure Mili that he had not given up music completely, he wrote that he had been playing the four-hand arrangements of symphonies with his brother, Philarète, and that he had read the scores of Gluck's *Alceste*, *Iphigenia in Aulis*, and *Armide*, and Mozart's Requiem. But of his own compositions, which were supposed to have included several songs, he spoke in rather vague terms except for mentioning that he had begun to compose a piano sonata.

Mili no doubt was flattered by Modeste's devotion to him, but he could not help being irritated by the jumble in his letters: "What utter rubbish! And how does he manage to reconcile faith in immortality of the soul with infusorial earth." Mili advised him to make a piano arrangement of the Persian Chorus from Glinka's opera *Russlan and Ludmilla*, and urged him to complete the sonata he had been talking about for so long.

There was something, however, that Modeste had managed to conceal, not only from his friends but also from Mili, who was then his closest confidant. Two years later in a letter to Mili he merely mentioned that he had been suffering from a "terrible illness," and that that was one of the reasons for his inability to work or even to see Mili.

But the nature of his illness has never been firmly established. If Modeste ever named it, Mili must have destroyed those letters, for he never spoke of it. Nevertheless, judging from Modeste's allusions to his "terrible illness," one comes to the supposition that Moussorgsky was an epileptic.

Such a diagnosis would serve as a key not only to many of his characteristics and to his "visionary" ability, but also to his whole life-style, his relationships with people, and his choice of close friends. Being conscious of "*it*," Modeste's extremely sensitive nature kept him from too close association with young women, who would have been shocked, frightened, or perhaps even repelled and certainly of no help if he were suddenly stricken with a seizure. It may explain the complete absence of any record of his love affairs, which for a young, handsome, and talented officer of an elite regiment would have been natural.

Thus, the few allusions to Moussorgsky's loves lack any evidence of a consummated love affair. According to one rumor, provided by Philarète, Modeste while still in his late teens fell in love with one of his cousins. The young girl died, and a package of his letters to her, so the story goes, was placed under her head in the coffin; thus the mystery of his first love was buried with her. The only proof of Modeste's feelings is ascribed to the first song he had composed—"Tell Me, Dear Little Star, Where Art Thou?"—written to a touching text of his own.

I would like to mention an episode that is supposed to have occurred at this period in Moussorgsky's life, according to a novel published in France in 1939.*

Modeste was supposed to have fallen in love with a prostitute appearing as a singer in a cheap nightclub along the river bank in St. Petersburg. Modeste was determined to

* Ivan Lukash, "*Le Pauvre amour de Moussorgsky.*" Adapted from Russian by Nadine d'Oblonska.

"rescue" the young woman, and even planned to marry her, but his hopes were thwarted. Once, while he was absent from his apartment (he presumably was living alone), the young woman was surprised by another woman who came to call on Moussorgsky. The "other" woman was of Modeste's own social class and the singer understood that her dream of becoming Moussorgsky's wife could never become a reality. She left Moussorgsky. He searched for her everywhere—so the story goes—and took to drink. Eventually he heard that she had drowned herself, but her image haunted him for the rest of his life.

On the first page of this novel is an author's note:

This is not a biography of Moussorgsky. This is a novel, but it might serve as a key to the mystery of his existence. A letter dated 1883 was found among the papers of a painter in St. Petersburg, which gives reason to believe in it.

This, however, is just as mysterious as "the mystery of his existence," for the author fails to give the name of the painter or of the writer of the letter.

The author continues in his note:

The contemporaries of Moussorgsky always spoke of a street singer, who accompanied herself on a harp in the nightclub frequented by Moussorgsky.

In my reading of all the documents, letters, and biographies concerning Moussorgsky, I have never seen a reference to the abovementioned person. The story reads like a motion-picture script that combines Dostoyevsky's Raskolnikov and Sonia Marmeladova (*Crime and Punishment*) and Tolstoy's Katusha Maslova and Prince Nekhludov (*The Resurrection*). The most that can be said of this tale is that it is possible, but not plausible.

Some of Moussorgsky's biographers are inclined to believe that the nineteenth-century Russians were often incapable of ever getting over their first loves, but such an assumption was certainly baseless in Moussorgsky's case.

The frequent recurrence of epileptic attacks during that particular period of his life would also explain his avoidance of his friends, even when he was on short visits to St. Petersburg. For weeks at a time nobody would know his whereabouts, until a letter, written in a cheerful tone as if nothing at all had happened, would indicate his temporary address.

❧ *Three* ❧

EVER since he had resigned from his regiment, Modeste
was his own master and could pass his time as he
chose. He often went to his family's estate in Karevo,
where he claimed that he was "thinking . . . thinking
. . . thinking"; or as soon as he felt an improvement in
his health, he would throw to the winds his own prescrip-
tion for a cure by keeping away from all musical activities
and visiting the Shilovskys at Glebovo, their luxurious estate near Moscow.

Modeste had met Maria Shilovskaya (*née* Verderov-
skaya) at Dargomizhsky's musicales. From the age of nine-
teen, Maria, daughter of a governor in Siberia, had been a
pupil of Dargomizhsky. Among a large number of other
men, Dargomizhsky was enamored not so much of Maria's
mezzo-soprano as of her exceptionally seductive appearance
and her charm. After a few "turbulent years"—the delicate
way in which her frequent love affairs were recorded—
Maria married Stepan Shilovsky, a former Guard officer,
though better known for his large fortune. Apparently his
gold outweighed the qualities and talents of his competitors

in the musical circles; while Maria for her part not only turned his head, she also turned his estate into a musical playground for her admirers. She had him build a theater, assemble an orchestra, and import professional singers from the capital to give performances of operas in which otherwise she could never have sung the title roles.

Although she was married and almost ten years older than he, Modeste was among those who never ceased to trail after her. And she accepted him in her entourage not only because he was young and handsome and eager to participate in all her projects, but because in addition to his musical talent he had already shown a remarkable feeling for acting.

He had played the role of a high-school teacher in Victor Krylov's one-act comedy *A Fair Copy*, which was performed to celebrate César Cui's wedding to Malvina Bamberg (October 8, 1858) at his father-in-law's apartment. A few months later Modeste played the role of a civil servant in Gogol's *The Lawsuit*, which was followed by a performance the same evening of Cui's early opera *The Mandarin's Son* in which Modeste sang the role of the Mandarin. "Moussorgsky played these roles with such adroitness and comic quality of diction, poise, and gesture that he made the audience roar with laughter," Stassov remarked later.

Maria would have been foolish not to make use of Modeste: he served her as an advisor on theatrical matters and on her amateurish composing, and she had entrusted him with coaching the chorus for opera performances—the first and last time Modeste appeared in the role of conductor.

Thus, Modeste was always welcome at the Shilovskys,

but it has never been ascertained whether his long visits there were for purely artistic purposes and enjoyment, or whether it was his hostess in whom his principal interest lay. Modeste, who usually expressed his emotions spontaneously and freely, kept silent about his feelings toward women. In his reports to Mili from the Shilovskys' estate he barely mentioned Maria, but some time afterwards he almost broke his rule by saying that he would tell Mili when he next saw him about a "woman affair." But he never kept this promise; and if there was anything between Maria and himself, as some have surmised, the only evidence of his obviously one-sided love affair was in a song he dedicated to her—"What Are the Words of Love to You?"—based on a poem by A. Amossov.

Perhaps because Mili disapproved of Modeste's relationship with the Shilovskys and considered the spending of so much time on their amateur performances as a waste of his energy, which he should have been devoting to his own serious work, Modeste, to assert his independence, was in no hurry to return to St. Petersburg. Or perhaps because Mili's name in relation to music was associated in Modeste's mind with Russian National Music, about which Stassov and Mili were constantly preaching to him, Modeste felt he had to go to Moscow to see the heart of Russia.

In Moscow, he hastened to report to Mili, he had noticed a remarkable thing: from the belfries and domes of the churches was wafted the breath of times long since past. As he walked toward the Kremlin and the Cathedral of Basil the Blessed—"those were the holy past"—he had almost expected a boyar to go by in a long kaftan and tall fur hat. In the Archangelsky Cathedral, when he examined the tombs of men who had been rulers of Russia, he thought of Glinka's *A Life for the Tsar*. He watched the beggars sitting on the stone steps leading to church entrances—"Such beggars and frauds the world has never seen," he remarked —and fascinated, he studied their weird gestures and grimaces, the fidgety convulsions of their bodies, and was amused by their nicknames for each other.

It reminded him that some fifteen generations back (in the fifteenth century) an ancestor named Roman had been nicknamed "Moussorga," "Bungler" (*mussor*, in Russian, means trash), though in slang it could also he interpreted as "Pockmarked." Modeste also heard of another interpretation of "Moussorga"—"Foul-mouthed." Thus Roman's son, through the use of the Russian genitive, was called Moussorgskoi or Moussorgsky. At any rate, Modeste liked the origin of his last name: it spoke of his kinship with the Russian people.

He was spellbound by the sight of Red Square. He vividly recalled many phases in the history of Russia which had been witnessed, he thought, by the old churches and ancient buildings. Lifting his eyes from the pavement over which Napoleon's Grande Armée had passed, first victorious and then defeated, he looked up at the Kremlin and could easily see the glow in the sky above the burning city which had summoned all Russians to stand together against the invader. His heart swelled with the pride of belonging to a nation that was ready to perish rather than surrender. It was good to feel its strength. It was good to be Russian. "I *was* cosmopolitan," he wrote Mili, "but now everything Russian is so close, so dear to me, that I would be very much annoyed if Russia were not properly respected in our time. It seems to me that I begin to love Russia."

Now he began to understand better and see more vividly what Russian National Music should reflect. He began to comprehend Balakirev's and Stassov's theories, which until then had been merely abstract ideas to him. He was eager to start composing, but upon his return to St. Petersburg he was still suffering from a recurrence of his illness. He avoided everybody except the Opochinins, Nadezhda and her brother Alexander, an amateur musician, whom he had met at Dargomizhsky's musicales. At their home he read with Nadezhda Alexander Herzen's novel *Who Is To Blame?*, which was then very popular among the intelligentsia, either because of its author or because of its romantic content.

Alexander Herzen is best known for his memoirs *My Thoughts and My Past* and for his support of the revolutionary and socialist movements in Europe during the second part of the last century to which he contributed through writing articles as well as through making generous donations from his large personal fortune. Having suffered arrest and exile twice, Herzen in 1847 at the age of thirty-five had settled in London, where he published in Russian *Kolokol* (*The Bell*), a periodical with the motto *Vivos Voco!*, aimed against the Russian monarchy and which was smuggled into Russia. Modeste knew about the magazine from Balakirev, who had heard frequent discussions of *Kolokol* at the Stassovs.

Who Is To Blame? was one of Herzen's first published works, a rather experimental attempt at writing a novel. And he was so discouraged by the reaction of friends, to whom he read the first part, that it was only because of the insistence of Vissarion Belinsky, the leading literary critic of the day, that Herzen completed his story. It was published in 1846 under the name of Iskander, a pseudonym Herzen often used later.

The novel has a simple plot. Vladimir Beltov, a man of independent means, falls in love with Lyuba Kruziferskaya who reciprocates his feelings, but their happiness is marred by the fact that Lyuba is married to Beltov's close friend, a schoolteacher. The novel ends with Beltov leaving the town, leaving Lyuba with only a dream of happiness that is never to be theirs.

The ambiguous title, *Who Is To Blame?*, has no direct answer in the novel. None of the characters in the triangular situation was to blame, but rather the general structure of Russian society before 1861. Like Pushkin's Evgeni Onegin, Tchulkaturin in Turgenev's *The Diary of a Superfluous Man*, and Rudin in his *Rudin*, Herzen portrayed in Beltov a "superfluous man," the victim of a feudal society in which he led a useless life. Provided with an income from their estates, which were worked by the peasants whom they "owned," such men lacked the initiative to pursue useful occupations; it led to a boring existence from which they found no escape, either in their sojourns abroad or upon their return to the same kind of life in Russia.

The twenty-year-old Modeste must have been particularly impressed by a dramatic "event" in the novel that took place in an arbor in the garden of a small provincial town at twilight on a warm April day. And indeed he was inspired by a scene against this romantic background to compose his Impromptu Passione: an animated discussion of their love between Beltov and Lyuba, crowned by a long and a passionate kiss—the one and only in their relationship.

On his manuscript was this inscription: "Dedicated to Nadezhda (Petrovna) Opochinina [and] to the memory of Beltov and Lyuba [the principal characters in the novel], October 1st, 1859." This was the first "official" mention of Opochinina's name, indicating Modeste's close friendship with a woman almost twenty years older than he. Their relationship, which had intensified during the years following, was terminated by Nadezhda's death in 1875; its intimacy has to be judged by inscriptions on several works he had dedicated to her.

His letters to Mili, with whom he used to share his plans and the progress of his work, were not as frequent, and almost a year had passed before he collected strength enough to write him. "My illness lasted until August [1860], so that I could devote myself to music only at brief intervals; most of the time from May to August my brain was weak and I was highly excitable." Nevertheless, he said, he wanted Mili to know that in addition to two choruses and an introduction to *Oedipus*—incidental music to Sophocles' tragedy which he was dedicating to Mili—he was very much preoccupied with *The Witches*, a drama by Baron Mengden. "A whole act is to take place on Bald Mountain," he wrote Mili: "a Witches' Sabbat, episodes of sorcery, a solemn march of all this *nastiness*, a finale—the glorification of the Sabbat in which Mengden introduces the commander of the whole festival on Bald Mountain." Although at that time he did not advance very far with his score, and Baron Mengden's drama remained in manuscript form, Modeste was to be haunted during the next six years by the vision of an orchestral composition describing the festival on Bald Mountain.

Modeste was restless. He went back to Moscow, where he planned to work and even hired a piano, but he soon discovered that it was not as simple as he had thought, and he did more talking about composing than actually getting to work. And he found ample opportunity for that. He joined a group of former university students, with whom he spent his evenings, as he reported to Mili, "in shaking down to their foundation history, the administration, chemistry, the arts—everything."

He enjoyed this so much that he was constantly postponing his return to St. Petersburg. Mili was annoyed with Modeste's erratic behavior. He had been very much against his friendship with the Shilovskys and his long visits on their estate, and now he favored even less his new Moscow acquaintances and their pastimes. In his letters Mili tried to convince Modeste that he was wasting his time, and even tried to have Philarète influence his younger brother. But Modeste paid no attention to them.

For a while Mili stopped writing to Modeste—it was not in his nature to coddle a child, and certainly not a problem child—and when he did write again, he didn't bother to restrain himself from criticizing what were, in his opinion, the limited interests of Modeste's new friends. It hurt Modeste's ego and pride, and he answered Mili with a saucy letter:

. . . In regard to the fact that I am sinking and that somebody has to pull me out, all I can say is that, given a talent, a man does not sink if his brain is working. If he has neither the one nor the other, there is no use pulling him out like an old splinter. It is about time that you stopped treating me like a child who has to be guided so that he won't fall. And as for my being attracted by "limited" people, all I can answer is "Tell me whom you love and I'll tell you who you are." Thus, logically, I am also very limited.

Mili did not think he was limited. Mili thought Modeste was a driveling idiot.

❧ *Four* ❧

MEANWHILE, two events were taking place in St. Petersburg, radically changing the lives and activities of Russian musicians. Even as late as 1860 musicians in Russia were not classified as belonging to any profession. There were no music schools or conservatories which, like the universities, could have provided their graduates with the officially recognized positions of music teachers or performers, as well as with a social status and its rights. Anton Rubinstein, then at the height of his fame and popularity as a concert pianist in Russia and abroad, finally succeeded in founding the first conservatory in Russia. His project was handsomely supported by the patronage of the Grand Duchess Elena Pavlovna through her influence at the court.

German by birth, educated in Germany and France, she had shown more energy and organizing talent than most men at the court, so that it was rumored that Czar Nicholas I was afraid of his sister-in-law. A great lover of music, she had already helped Rubinstein in forming the first Russian Musical Society (1858) to present symphonic concerts, and now she was particularly sympathetic to his plan of establishing a conservatory whose methods were to be similar to those of German conservatories.

That was the beginning of a feud between the Russian musicians who were oriented toward Western Europe, and the nationalists, who firmly believed that it was "high time to stop borrowing ideas from abroad, high time to have their own."

It stirred the nationalists to indignation and heated discussions, and incited Stassov, their mouthpiece, into writing vitriolic articles that ridiculed the whole idea of teaching *à la German*, in addition to attacking Rubinstein personally. Stassov accused him of always capitalizing on his title of piano virtuoso, first by having performed his unworthy compositions at the Musical Society's symphonic concerts and now as a self-appointed champion of Russian culture. He implied that Rubinstein, as a Jew, was no representative of the Russian people, and listing the names of the proposed choice for the faculty—Preyschock, Madame Nissen-Salomon, Wieniawsky, Leschetizky—said, "Not a single Russian in the whole lot."

Mili Balakirev, on the other hand, was not satisfied with mere criticism, and to counteract the establishment of the conservatory, he set out to organize the Free Music School. In contrast with the conservatory, this school was to be *free* in the absolute meaning of the word: there were to be no tuitions, no teachers' salaries, no homework and no examinations, and lectures were to be open free of charge to persons of all professions.

The two schools differed simply because the conservatory was well endowed with funds procured by the Grand

Duchess, while the Free Music School was also "free" of any substantial financial support. Thus, the conservatory was to have classes in every branch of musical education, while the Free Music School could afford to teach only choral singing. But since the conservatory was in a way affiliated with the symphonic concerts given under Rubinstein's direction at the Russian Musical Society, the Free Music School was to give its own public performances conducted by Mili Balakirev.

Modeste Moussorgsky could not lend his helping hand in this controversy, for a far more significant factor had affected his life: Through Balakirev's occasional references to political discussions at the Stassovs', Modeste had gradually been acquiring a comprehensive view of the political situation in Russia. "I am handing you the command of the country when it is in a poor state," the dying Nicholas I said to his son Alexander II, while Russia was losing the Crimean War. The Russian people were blaming the authorities for the humiliating defeat and the loss of Russia's prestige as a military power. They had neither forgiven nor forgotten the cruel way in which the December Revolution of 1825 had been crushed and the ruthless treatment of public opinion by the police and censorship during Nicholas I's reign, which, nevertheless, for the first time had made itself felt in the newspapers and periodicals, as well as in the works of the foremost Russian authors. All of them clamored for reforms, a new code of law, the institution of jury trial, higher education, and—above all—the abolition of serfdom.

In his periodical *The Contemporary*, Nikolai Chernyshevsky (1825–1868), a writer and a liberal political leader who steadily was gaining a large following among the members of the intelligentsia, called for a great reform movement to bring about a "rational distribution of the economic wealth" through the abolition of serfdom.

Alexander II, who succeeded Nicholas I, was a weaker character than his father. "Better that the reform come from above than wait until serfdom is abolished from below," he admitted, but his first plan (January 1858) for an agrarian reform aroused the landlords to a not unexpected wrath.

"Hamlet's dilemma—to be or not to be—is facing us—sinners," the liberally minded Ulibishev reported sarcastically in his letter to Mili Balakirev. "All the owls, bats, and vampires from eleven districts flew into town [Nizhni-Novgorod, one of the oldest "nests" of Russian nobility] with weeping and howling that rend your heart, for it seems that someone wants to tear from their claws the human prey on which they have fed for so long. *Hélas! Hélas! Hélas!!!* It is impossible to suck from the peasants the last drop of their blood, and then sell their flesh. 'We won't have it, we won't have it' [the planned agrarian reform], scream our noblemen."

Ulibishev had already acquainted his serfs with the coming reform, but he did not live to see them freed, for he died in 1858.

At first Modeste was bewildered and looked up to Balakirev, in whose intellectual superiority he had an almost blind faith, for clarification of the whole situation. But Mili himself was no less bewildered. His background—the pro-

vincial Nizhni-Novgorod middle class—stood in the way of
his fully comprehending such slogans as "Go to the people,
learn about the people." Mili was a musician, an individual-
ist; he knew nothing about "the people." Stassov, on the
other hand, with whom he had long discussions on the subject, had a great faith in "the people," and, repeating his
argument for the necessity of creating a Russian National
Music, advised Mili to read carefully Chernyshevsky's recently published (1855) *The Aesthetic Relation of Art to
Reality*. (It served later as a basis for Tolstoy's similar
views.)

As a musician Mili understood this, but as far as the
general agrarian reform was concerned, he was of no help
to Modeste. Modeste soon had to learn the whole problem
at first hand. By the manifesto of February 19, 1861, Czar
Alexander II had abolished serfdom. It impoverished the
landowners, including the Moussorgskys.

Their father had died, and Philarète and Modeste were
not particularly competent in managing their estates. With
their income thus drastically reduced they had to give up
their spacious St. Petersburg apartment and their mother
had to return permanently to Karevo, where Modeste had
to go to administer whatever could be salvaged from their
estates.

Modeste had never before had to give a thought to
money, which was derived from the land and the serfs who
worked it. He had always had ample means for a completely independent life, but now he was faced with problems unfamiliar to him and alien to his nature. He reported
to Cui:

It is all so tedious, dreary, annoying—the Devil knows what!
The caretaker [of the estate] played such a dirty trick! I had
intended to do some decent work—instead of which, if you
please, I am to make investigations, get information, run to the
police and civil courts. . . . If my mother were not here, these
fools would drive me mad. It is only for her sake that I stay on;
it makes her happy to have me with her, and I am glad to be
able to give her this pleasure.

Oh, but what "planters" these landlords are! They are very
proud of the club they have organized in the little town, and
they meet there almost daily to get boisterous. The proceedings
usually begin with a speech, followed by some sort of general
announcement for the benefit of these "gentlemen," and nearly
always end in a fight so that you feel like sending for the police.
And all this goes on in an "aristocratic" club and these are the
gentry with whom one has to associate every day! Day after
day they tearfully carry on over their "lost rights" and "total
ruin" with howling and gnashing of teeth and violent scenes. If
you give these "aristocrats" the right to meet, they meet; if you
give them the right to argue about their business, they argue—
and at that with fists and obscene language. True, the younger
fellows are more decent, but I never see them; it is they who
negotiate with the peasants and are therefore always on the
road. And this is the fetid atmosphere in which I have to live
and breathe. It certainly does not appeal to the artistic instincts!
A man has enough to do to prevent the stink from choking him.
How can anybody think about music?

And indeed, during the following years his music was
almost silent. And yet eventually it profited by his long stay
in the country. Philarète was extremely scornful of
Modeste's attitude toward the abolishment of serfdom. In
fact, with the superior air of an elder brother he thought
that Modeste was now reaping the fruits of his belief that

serfs should be granted the civil rights enjoyed by everybody else. But Modeste then had an opportunity to familiarize himself even more with the peasants—the Russian people.

The peasants are far more capable of self-government than the landlords are. At their meetings they conduct matters directly and to the point, and in their own way discuss their interests in a very businesslike manner, while the landlords, when *they* meet, quarrel and show off their ambitions, quite forgetting the purpose of the meeting. This is consoling, for it puts a trump card into our hands.

His saying "our hands" clearly indicated his sympathy with the peasants' cause. It confirmed his wholehearted agreement with *Narodnichestvo* and the reforms advocated by Alexander Herzen's *Kolokol*. These were the seeds of Moussorgsky's political conception, which today would be called socialist.

As once before he had studied the behavior of beggars sitting on the steps of Moscow churches, now he analyzed the characteristics of former serfs. It took them some time to overcome their suspicion when he, their former landlord and master, wanted to join them in their work in the fields and later with the harvesting. He moved to a straw-thatched hut, rising "with the roosters" and going to bed when the cows were brought back to their stalls. Working side by side with the peasants, he also studied their particularly colorful speech—in fact, he was learning at close range that "truth" about the Russian people which he intended to portray in his compositions.

One of his early instrumental works, Intermezzo Symphonique in modo classico, was inspired by a rural scene he

had witnessed on a sunny winter day. A crowd of peasants
was crossing the fields with difficulty through the snowdrifts, many of them repeatedly falling into the snow and
then scrambling upward. Suddenly, a group of young
peasant women appeared in the distance, laughing and
singing. Modeste later told Stassov as he explained his
composition, "This was picturesque, serious, but amusing."
And although its main melodies and the form of composition were in modo classico, Modeste confided to Stassov that
he believed that the Intermezzo was "secretly" Russian.

Philarète was gone on business to St. Petersburg, Yulia
was away visiting her relatives, and Modeste, not to remain
alone in Karevo, went to the village of Volok, in Pskov
Province. He remained there at the home of Natalia Kosho-
lova from the beginning of March until May 1862. Shortly
after his arrival he wrote to Mili (March 11, 1862).

I am splendidly situated, so far in good health and in comparatively good spirits.

I lead the life of a respectable person—go to bed at eleven,
rise at eight and this schedule is proving very pleasant to me.
Snow, wind and frost. I wait with impatience for spring—to
begin the cure—it's time to start my brain working, let's stop
deluding ourselves. I must work, I must do things, and one can
do it only when one feels well; in a delirious condition one can
only tremble, create fantasies, and squander one's strength in
vain—in its way it is a kind of spiritual masturbation. . . .

When one changes one's atmosphere and surroundings—one
feels refreshed; the past becomes purified, standing in bold
relief, and then one can analyze what one has lived through.
Having realized this now that I've gone to the country, I see
that although I haven't run away from work, I have—with my
Russian laziness—done little; I do not have any particular faith
in my talent, although I don't have any doubt of it; therefore,

I want to work according to my strength, and I will, but I am searching for other activities where I would make myself useful. Moreover, I am discovering in myself something that is already obvious—a kind of looseness, a weakness, you called it doughiness, I now recall, and I was a little hurt, because dough has the quality of retaining the impression of *dirty* fingers as well as *clean* ones. However, I intend to get rid of this weakness, it knocks me out; I now feel this clearly, because I want to do things.

Three weeks later Modeste wrote to Mili:

As soon as I got settled in this country place, I wrote you. But I've had no answer from you. I remain ignorant of the reason for your silence—I write a second epistle.

While my landlady's children forcefully bang their fingers on the keyboard, creating all imaginable *accords possibles et impossibles* (this is called taking music lessons; doing *this* they interfere with my music), I am reading a very interesting thing concerning nature in general and human nature particularly. The book bears the title *De la philosophie de la nature,** and what is pleasant is that it doesn't smell of that philosophic narrowness and the dogma of various philosophic gangs. This book is written by a *human being*, one who expounds his thoughts freely, lucidly, and with a great knowledge of the subject. Besides this, it has historical interest of the gradual development of man's knowledge of nature. After the first revolution the book was sentenced in France (by the *stinking stupidity* of Catholics and despots, dictators and presidents) to the auto-da-fe. O Frenchmen! O republicans! As usual the greater number of the copies was saved, before the stupid sentence could be carried out.

In consequence of the approach of spring and the impossibility of communication I am confined to my *petit réduit*. My company consists of a *hot-blooded* Prussian—tutor of my

* By Claude Izouard Delisle de Sales (1769).

landlady's children—a clear and well-developed brain, a remarkably energetic and alert gentleman. His Spartan character makes him useful to me: I am losing my Athenian flabbiness because he drags me through snowdrifts up to my waist, insisting that my "half-stupor" is due to the sluggish blood circulation and that my organism requires regular jolts until it *strengthens itself*. These *promenades monstres* really help me.

My Prussian plays the piano quite well and has some understanding of musical matters. He sometimes treats me to Bach's little fugues and of these the one in E *together* with its prelude pleases me especially—fortunately he plays it well. (The piano is a half-tone below pitch—the fugue sounds in E-flat major —I don't like E major.)

I often sound out my companion and on many subjects I find him, in his opinions, sympathetic. I confess I've begun to doubt my opinions in regard to Germans in Russia and Germans in general (except for the scholars and artists, who, naturally, have their own stature). As a German in Russia he, of course, is an exception to the *beer-drinking burgherdom* with Riga cigars. On my birthday (March 16) he showed himself at his most zealous. Before I had time to awake, I received some verses with a rosebud pinned to them—*a spring rose*. Poetry! Metaphors! (Oh so German!) *A thorough German!* The verses were not without a certain power—the author was too sensible to spare me with a rose, so they didn't turn out too badly.

Through newspaper reports and correspondence with his friends Modeste kept abreast with the events that stirred his colleagues in St. Petersburg. And when he heard about the first concerts conducted by Mili at the Free Music School at the end of March, 1862, he wrote him

I am delighted with the success of the two concerts, and may the newborn school grow great and prosper! . . . I find a free and unforced development of natural aptitudes which is sure to be more fresh and sound, incomparably more sympathetic than any scholastic or dramatic drill. . . . Just think what the professors cram into the young heads, and what one has to throw away as unnecessary and retain the essential!

Thus theorizing and as if he were telling Mili something Mili did not know, he gave a sarcastic description of the members of the conservatory faculty as compared with those at the Free Music School:

One is a den of professors; the other a free society devoted to art. In one place Zaremba [a teacher of composition] and Tupinstein [*tupoy*, in Russian, means stupid], clad in their anti-musical professorial togas, fill the heads of their pupils with every sort of vile rubbish and infect them at the very beginning. The unfortunate pupils see before them not human beings but posts with some sort of silly scribble written on them as musical rules. Rubinstein is dull, therefore he conscientiously performs his duties by maliciously stupefying the others. Not so Zaremba, a cunning fellow he, the very man to take the measurements of art by inches. Having been elevated to the dignity of *Doctor* (he is really more like a cobbler in an academic nightcap) he is not so childish and simple as to have views and give counsels on musical logic and esthetics. Not he! He has been taught the rules! And with this lymph he inoculates every aspirant against free learning.

As for Aunty Aleona [the Grand Duchess], I suppose she will not live as long as Methuselah; as a scourge she is but temporary. She is very unstable in her adoration and hatred, playful and always amorous. She is famous for her fickleness.

In the other school we have *you!* What more is there to say? All that is new, free, and powerful is yours by nature. Mankind needs such men. All success therefore, and a happy future to your splendid work!

Modeste was very anxious to be with his friends, but his diminished income prevented any long stay in the capital.

After consulting their mutual friends, Mili offered him their financial assistance, but Modeste refused to accept it. Even when he was as poor as a beggar, Moussorgsky was as proud as Peter the Great. In fact he had relinquished his share of their income to Philarète, who married in 1863. "He will need it more than I," Modeste reasoned. "He will have a family, and I . . . I can always manage to get by."

Influenced by the prevailing trend among the intelligentsia advocating that everyone do some useful work as a contribution to the newly acquired evidence of the government's more liberal attitude, Modeste eventually succeeded in obtaining a small post in the engineering department of the Ministry of Communications.

Thus, Modeste, who five years earlier had resigned from Russia's most elite regiment because he could not combine military duties with his work as a composer, now accepted a desk job that afforded even less material advantage and free time. This was hardly a position to make him "useful to society"—his qualifications were not of particular value to the department, and if he were employed at all, it was only through the good offices of his old friend Alexander Opochinin.

By adding to the meager salary whatever was left of his former resources, he was confident of having a comfortable living in St. Petersburg. He was eager to rejoin Mili's musical circle, which he heard had two new members. During his previous short visits to the capital he had already met at Mili's the young midshipman in the Naval Academy, Mili's latest musical discovery, Nikolai Rimsky-Korsakov.

The seventeen-year-old Nikolai (born in 1844) belonged to the naval Rimsky-Korsakov family, and although

like Modeste and Cui, he had shown an unusual talent and
interest in music, he too had had to follow family tradition
and had joined the Navy. So far Nikolai had not composed
a single note and played the piano badly, but his youthful
enthusiasm for music was sufficient to gain Mili's faith in
him. Mili drew him into the group of musicians who met
once a week at his home, where their mature discussions of
music and the arts captivated Nikolai so completely that
although he did not abandon the service for a long time,
music was to be his main interest in life.

At one of these evenings Modeste also had seen Alexander Borodin, whom he had met twice previously. Shortly
after Modeste had received his commission at the Preobrazhensky Regiment he was on duty in a military hospital
where Borodin, five years older and several inches taller
than himself (Borodin was over six feet tall), was working
as a doctor of medicine. Both men soon found a common
topic of conversation, for both were music enthusiasts, although contributing nothing to it as yet.

Borodin was the illegitimate son of the Georgian Prince
Luka Gedeonoshvili from whom he had inherited his dark
Oriental eyes and a sleepiness in his manner. He was regis-
tered under the name Borodin, that of one of his father's
serfs. As a boy he had learned to play the piano, cello, and
flute, and had even dabbled in composition, but he was far
too preoccupied with experiments in chemistry to regard
music as anything more important than a pleasant diversion.

Three years later, in the autumn of 1859, Modeste saw
Borodin again at the home of a doctor attached to an artil-
lery regiment. This time, for the benefit of the doctor's

guests, Modeste played with Borodin the four-hand arrangement of Mendelssohn's Symphony in A minor. Modeste impressed Borodin so much with his criticism of the Andante movement, which he considered nothing else than another "Song without Words," and with the descriptions of his own compositions, that Borodin was too bashful to even mention *his* attempts at composing.

Now meeting Borodin again at Mili's Modeste had behind him his military career and a few years of the carefree life, but he had gained in self-assurance and considered himself a professional composer, while Borodin had studied chemistry at the University of Heidelberg, had married, and had recently returned to St. Petersburg to accept the post of professor at the Academy of Medicine. Borodin was intimidated by the presence of professional musicians, and when asked to play some of his compositions, excused himself, saying, "I am only a Sunday composer who strives to remain obscure."

But Mili was not a man who could easily be put off by such a statement. "This is chemistry, this is medicine!" Mili said later to his friends, raising his forefinger. "A man of a certain age and position, with a small respectable belly, who wears gold epaulettes on feast days," and he enrolled Borodin as the fifth member of his group, which was to create a Russian National Music.

But when Modeste finally returned to St. Petersburg at the end of 1862, Mili was in the Caucasus, Rimsky-Korsakov was on a long sea voyage, Cui was engrossed in his growing family, his military service, and his current compositions, while Borodin was too busy at the Academy to spare any time for long discussions with Modeste. And

Modeste was thirsting for company after his long seclusion
in the country. Thus, he was reduced to occasional visits
with Stassov which he soon found most disappointing.
Modeste was extremely sensitive and felt that Stassov
thought very little of him. And he was not mistaken, for
Stassov wrote to Mili:

What is there for me in Moussorgsky? Well, yes, he seems to
agree with me, and yet I have not heard from him a single idea
or a single word expressed with a real profundity of understanding. Everything about him is flabby and colorless. To me
he seems a perfect *idiot.* Yesterday I could have flogged him. I
believe that if he were left without tutelage, if he were suddenly
removed from the sphere where you have held him by force,
and he were set free to follow his own wishes and his own
tastes, he would soon be overrun with weeds like all the rest.
There is nothing inside him. . . .

Mili was already of the same opinion and no longer tried
to "guide" Modeste, who was indeed going his own way,
"following his own wishes and his own tastes."

In Russia every great event—a victorious war or disastrous defeat, an uprising or famine or epidemic—always
brought men, particularly young men, close together so
that they could satisfy their exasperating need for expressing themselves. They were avid for information, anxious to
exchange new ideas and develop new theories. Striving to
solve social problems that had arisen from the recent reforms, they studied economics, history, and science. They
saw ahead of them a desired "truth" and behind them the
dark injustice for which society as a whole was *to blame.*
Differences of opinions brought even more interest into
their lives, kept their minds more vigorous, and helped

them to progress. Small circles sprang up all over the country, and not all of them, even in the eyes of the government, were of a revolutionary character; they offered such cooperation of thought and diversity of opinion that it made men out of mere youngsters.

Three years previously, while he was in Moscow, Modeste had already had a taste of such meetings of minds, but now he had joined a small group, which formed a community and lived in the same apartment. Each of the six members of this *Commune*, as they jokingly called it, had his own room, which except by special permission was closed to the rest. A large common room was reserved for their meals and recreation, and there they met in the evenings to converse, argue, read, or listen to Moussorgsky's playing the piano or singing songs and excerpts from operas.

All of them were well educated and intelligent, and in spite of their diverse services at the Senate or one of the ministries, each practiced his preferred scientific or artistic interest. Ideas that had been worked out by each became the property of all, and there was nothing so insignificant in any sphere of knowledge, in literature or art, that it was not communicated at once to every member of the *Commune*. Modeste Moussorgsky considered these three years of his life as his best: the exchange of ideas, of knowledge, of impressions from their reading all accumulated for him material on which he throve for the rest of his life; the principles of "justice," of "good" and "evil" as conceived and formed, remained axioms.

They read Gustave Flaubert's novel *Salammbo*, which appeared in a Russian translation in 1862, and Modeste was so impressed by its poetry and Oriental quality that he immediately began working on an opera based on it. This was his second attempt at a composition in this form; the first, based on Victor Hugo's *Han d'Ilande*, he had had to abandon because, as he said later, he did not know enough at the time to compose an opera.

Influenced by Richard Wagner's belief that an ideal composer is his own librettist, Modeste wrote the libretto, freely including verses by Heinrich Heine, Vasily Zhukovsky, Apollon Maikov, and other Russian poets. What remains of the score on which he frequently returned to work before giving up the project in 1866, shows his meticulous notes on decor, costumes, and stage directions. And yet it was the Oriental quality that had originally inspired him which was the main reason for his discouragement. He finally concluded that one cannot "invent the Orient," but that one had to have seen it and to be intimately acquainted with its atmosphere and spirit.

He was far happier in composing such works in the true Russian spirit as "Calistratus," written for voice with piano accompaniment on a text by Nikolai Nekrassov—"the poet of the poor, the wretched, and the forsaken." He dedicated this composition to Nadezhda Opochinina and marked the score "A first attempt at humorous music." But his sarcasm was more like Dostoyevsky's than Gogol's, for he wrote a gay melody in which Calistratus compared the carefree life predicted in his mother's lullaby with the wretched reality of his present life—his poverty, his wife and children in rags.

César Cui, far from appreciating Modeste's *tableau de genre musicale*, as Cui called "Calistratus" in his letter to

Mili, said, "All this is not devoid of some good harmonies and thoughts, but as a whole it is rather ridiculous." And two months later, answering Mili's letter, Cui said, ". . . You are much too hard on Modinka [Modeste]. To be indignant with him is impossible, but not to pity him is difficult." But Dargomizhsky was pleased with the composition, especially since he considered "humour in music" as his own original idea. Modeste may have been regarded as Mili's pupil, but he was more inclined to discover and develop Dargomizhsky's precepts of "truth" in music.

Modeste's happy life in the *Commune*, however, was dealt a severe blow. His mother was suffering from an illness from which she never recovered, and Modeste went to Karevo to be at her side. Shortly before her death in February, 1865, he composed, on Mikhail Lermontov's poem "A Prayer," a ballad for voice with piano accompaniment, which he dedicated to her.

With his mother's death Modeste lost his closest friend with whom, ever since his childhood, he had shared every moment of happiness, and in whom, when discouraged, he had found moral support. Their Karevo estate had to be auctioned. It was Modeste's last link with the fifteen generations of the Moussorgskys' seat. Modeste no longer had a home he could call his own. What was evident to everybody who knew him was that he was desperately lonely and that he was nearing a complete breakdown.

He despised his office work, a part of the government's administration that had been invented, in his opinion, to give a foretaste of "the frying pans in purgatory." Not even the lofty discussions with his friends in the *Commune* could

distract him, and he looked more and more often to a bottle
of alcohol to rescue him from the depressing reality of his
situation. Time and time again he wrote short notes to Mili
asking to be excused from his weekly meetings, concerts, or
opera performances. "My nervous trouble is working up
again in the most unpleasant manner, and I am forced to
watch it very carefully. To ward off a bad attack I intend to
remain quietly at home and rest. . . ."

Modeste's tormented and often beclouded mind dwelt on
memories of his mother, his childhood, and his old nurse
and her bedtime stories. He composed two short piano
pieces, from memories of childhood—"My Nurse and I"
and "First Punishment" (Nurse shut me in a dark room)—
and "Sleep, Sleep, Peasant's Son," a lullaby based on a text
from Alexander Ostrovsky's "The Voyevoda." He dedicated
both compositions to his mother's memory.

During that "difficult" year of 1865 he also composed
"The Outcast," based on the text written by one of his
friends in the commune.

> Look not on her to despise her,
> turn not away from her so.
> They are more blessed and wiser
> who can forgive, for they know.

The reference to a "fallen woman" was equally significant
for himself and his drinking.

More and more often Modeste had to be excused from
his office for a period of three or four weeks for, as it was
called, "domestic circumstances." He drank constantly, even
to the point of delirium tremens, when once more he was

stricken with epileptic fits. He was in urgent need of rest and care, which neither the commune nor his musical friends could offer him. Fortunately Philarète, who until then had shown no interest in his brother, rescued him by taking Modeste home to live with his family.

❧ *Five* ❧

THE following three years, which Modeste spent under the care of Philarète and his wife, were very beneficial for his health. During the winters he lived with them at their apartment in St. Petersburg, and in the summers they moved to Minkino, one of the estates still in Philarète's possession. There, on Minkino Farm, he led what he called the life of a "gentleman farmer." He worked in the fields, as he had done before in Karevo, canned, even made jam (an obligatory item on a Russian tea table), and lent a hand with the harvesting. The outdoor life helped his health and spirits to recover quickly, and by September of that first summer in the country he had composed "Savishna," a ballade for voice with piano accompaniment based on his own text.

It is a musical sketch portraying an episode he had witnessed from the window of his room: a wretched feebleminded young peasant was begging a beautiful girl not to reject his love. Limping as he followed her, he implored her to have mercy on one whom a cruel fate had made the subject of ridicule and humiliation in the village.

Modeste was so deeply moved that it took him some time before he could bring himself to conceive the musical image of the tragic scene he wished to convey. Finally he created the portrait of a *yurodivyi*, a half-witted imbecile well-known in Russian villages who, incapable of work, lived on the bounty of the peasants because they believed that God spoke through him. The *yurodivyi* spoke that "truth" which Modeste had been seeking to express in his compositions.

But like the love of his hero in the ballad, Moussorgsky's piece was rejected by Mili. Admitting some merit in "Savishna," he still insisted that Modeste needed guidance in his work; and Cui, to whom the composition was dedicated, said that it was absurd to expect anyone to sing in $\frac{5}{4}$ time, thus completely missing Modeste's thoroughly original device for illustrating *yurodivyi*'s limping and stuttering.

Nevertheless, it was the first composition to bring an indisputable recognition of Modeste's talent. Alexander Serov, one of the severest critics of the Balakirev group, wrote, "An impressive scene. Moussorgsky is the Shakespeare of music."

Even Stassov, who only recently had been ready to give Modeste a sound thrashing for his brooding, now, after having heard his "Outcast" and "Savishna" reversed his opinion of Modeste's talent so much that whenever Moussorgsky (after his return from the country) would go to the piano, Stassov would significantly nod at everybody present, and with an "oh" and "ah" as soon as Modeste began to play, was ready to shout "Hurrah" before he came to the end of his piece.

But as Cui justly pointed out over and over again, the Balakirev group, despite all their discussions of theories and plans for Russian National Music, still lacked a single major composition to illustrate their principles. Thus, when Nikolai Rimsky-Korsakov returned from his two-year sea voyage bringing only a fragmentary version of a symphony, it was timely and most welcome.

Mili set feverishly to work with Rimsky-Korsakov on the score, to which the twenty-two-year-old composer still had to add some material before the whole could be orchestrated and prepared for a performance in December, 1865.

It was an exciting event for the Balakirev group, and a historical one for Russian National Music. Rimsky-Korsakov's symphony was hailed for its simplicity, free development of ideas, and various forms. In fact, it was so close to Glinka's precept for a national music, that it was generally accepted as the first truly Russian symphony.

The Balakirev group gained prestige and a new member for popularizing their cause. Glinka's sister Ludmilla Shestakova, a fifty-year-old widow, opened her home for meetings, to be held in addition to those at Mili's, and from that day Modeste more than the others enjoyed her hospitality and her warm affectionate attitude. "Like a cat," he said, "I always return to her home."

Since *A Life for the Tsar* and *Russlan and Ludmilla*, although rejected in Russia always remained as the cornerstones of a national music, the Balakirev group was determined to resurrect them, even if it had to be done abroad. With Shestakova's patronage and her personal intervention in the negotiations with the directors of the Prague Opera, Mili succeeded in arranging performances of Glinka's operas in Prague in 1867. It was going to be the first presentation of a Russian opera outside Russia. Mili's friends were exuberant, and Stassov wrote a flamboyant article, hailing a new era in the history of Russian music.

Bitter disappointment in the Prague production followed, and no one was more sympathetic than Modeste with Mili's difficulties in trying to introduce Russian music to the Czechs, who had contributed their singers, chorus, orchestra, and decor. And no one was more explicit in his wrath against the "little Slav brothers" than Modeste in his letters to Mili which accused the Czechs of being totally Germanized.

. . . Your letter to Cui confirms what I thought—that your life in Prague is not very pleasant now, and the Devil knows it was miserable before. I confess that when you left for Czechia, I thought (in fact I knew) that the gracious invitations you had received had come from a select group, which was as it should have been. But I was wrong in my judgment of the degree of influence these few had on the Czech people. It seems now that among all two-footed Czech animals one can find only three who have the right to belong to the human race. And as though just to be malicious about your arrival in Prague, Pan Moniuszko scurried there with his Catholic operas. This combination of the Polish clique and German academic stupidity is a fruit that makes one vomit. How delighted I should be if after your conducting of *A Life for the Czar* and *Russlan*, such an impression would be made on the people that all these . . . [Here Moussorgsky changed the names of the Czech composers in such a way that, though the words sound like names, they represent something derogatory in Russian: sour cream,* bad shoemaker, scoundrel, corruption] would choke on their own works —the Devil take them! However, all this is easy to say or to write, but one doesn't get anywhere that way. . . .

Archimedes invented a level for his system which could

* For instance, if the accent is put on the second syllable of "Smetana," the name would mean "sour cream" in Russian.

turn the earth on its axis, and he was *killed by a Roman soldier,* but if Archimedes should propose to put the Czech brain onto the right track, he would certainly burst in vexation *even if he weren't killed by a Roman soldier.* —Is it possible that our music has to be limited by our borders—from the west along the Baltic Sea, Prussia, Galicia, and so on, to the south on the Black Sea and so on, to the east and north—in a word, according to geography? Is it possible that among people of our own race our national music cannot be grafted? Just remember that in all Europe two principles govern music—vogue and slavery. The English import singers and perform works—both of them outrageous—but there they follow the vogue. The French—oh well, the French have their *cancan, "Debarassez-nous de M. Berlioz!"* ("Deliver us from M. Berlioz!") The Spaniards, Italians, Turks, and Greeks we can ignore. As for the Germans, the best example of their musical slavery is their adoration of the conservatory and routine—beer and stinking cigars, music and beer, stinking cigars and music *ins Grüne!* The German is capable of producing a whole treatise on the way Beethoven wrote a quarter-note with the tail up instead of down, and how this should have been written correctly according to the rules. Once a German recognizes a *genius,* he becomes his slave. He cannot imagine that Beethoven, while writing fast, perhaps made a mistake or paid no attention to such a trifle.

This stupid and dead side of a beer's belly *mit Milch und süsse Suppe* is revolting enough in a true German, but it is even more revolting in those slaves of slaves, the Czechs, who refuse to wear their own physiognomy.

I spin all this out, dear Mili, because I am furious over the position in which you are placed among these dumb animals, and enraged by these Germans, Italians, and Jews, who here in Russia bamboozle our honest, good-natured, naïve Russians. Nobody could characterize the Czechs better than you do; though you look through musical lenses, the picture is the same. If you try to force me to sing (not in jest) Mendel's [Mendelssohn's] songs, I, a gentle and refined man, will become a mannerless ruffian. If you try to force a Russian muzhik to love any kind of putrefied German folksong, he will never do it. If you offer (not force—because you can force a German Czech to swallow Austrian spittle and he *will* swallow it) to sweeten a Czech's soul with tainted German provisions, he will sweeten it and say aloud that he is a Slav. This is how I understood the Czechs from your description, and these living corpses dared to listen to a Slav's creations, dare to demand Slavic music. . . . People or society who do not feel those sounds, which, like the memory of one's own mother or a close friend, make all the life strings in human beings vibrate, which would awaken them from their deep slumber and make them comprehend their own individuality, and the yoke they bear that is gradually killing this individuality—such society, such people are corpses. And the select members of such society are the doctors, who, with an electrogalvanic current, made the members of this corpse jerk before it starts to disintegrate chemically.

Jews are deeply moved by their own songs, which come down to them from one generation to the next. Their eyes burn with honest, not pecuniary, fire. I have myself been a witness to this. Jews are better than Czechs—I mean our own Jews, those who come from Bialostok, Lutsk, and Nevil, who live in dirty, stinking huts.

Could one say that a Slavic sound did not touch the Slavic soul because Smetana soured a sound? A lie! He couldn't cripple the opera to such a degree that it wouldn't have one live moment which would stir a living human being. Corpses sat in the theater, a corpse conducted an orchestra of corpses, and you, my dear, went to a Prague diversion *des revenants. One man alive among the dead.* I sympathize with you, my dear Mili, in your gloomy situation, and I should be proud of you if just for an hour you could bring these corpses to life. . . .

(71)

But by the time Mili returned home the "little Slav brothers" had to be forgiven, for all members of the large Slav family were coming to attend the first Pan-Slavic Committee organized in St. Petersburg. To celebrate the occasion, Mili conducted a symphonic concert, which featured works extended to compliment their guests. Starting with Glinka's Kamarinskaya, representing Russia, and Dargomizhsky's Kazachok, the Ukraine, he continued with his own Fantasy on Czech Themes and Rimsky-Korsakov's Serbian Fantasy, which had been written in record time, and closed the evening's program with Moniuszko's Polonaise.

Although neither Borodin, Cui, nor Moussorgsky was represented on this program, when Stassov wrote his review, he made the following remark: "Let us hope that our Slav guests will remember how much poetry, feeling, talent, and ability the small but already mighty heap of Russian musicians bring." This reference to a "small but already mighty heap" was repeated by the press so often that it became a nickname for the Balakirev group. Together with Balakirev, Borodin, Cui, and Rimsky-Korsakov, Modeste was included in this "mighty heap." (The "Mighty Five" is the free English adaptation of this nickname.)

By 1868 Philarète's finances had suffered such a setback that he had to give up his St. Petersburg apartment and move to the country for good, thus leaving Modeste without a place to stay during the winter months. Several of his friends offered him their hospitality, and he chose the Opochinins' whenever he came to the capital.

Modeste was in much better health, was awaiting another post promised by Alexander Opochinin, and meanwhile resumed his visits to Dargomizhsky's circle, which had radically changed during the past few years.

After spending a year traveling in Europe, where he had hoped to find solace for the disappointment he felt from the failure of his operas in Russia, Dargomizhsky returned home, freed himself from his former followers, whose flattery no longer pleased him, and, retaining a few friends of old standing, he welcomed the "Mighty Five" to his customary musicales.

There Modeste met for the first time the two Purgold sisters: the twenty-five-year-old Alexandra, who had studied singing under Henrietta Nielson-Solomon, a member of the St. Petersburg Conservatory, and her twenty-year-old sister, Nadezhda, a pianist and pupil of Anton Herke, Modeste's former piano teacher. The two young women had seven brothers and one sister and, at one time, with their parents, their nurses, tutors, and domestic help, they all lived in a large apartment, just one floor above Dargomizhsky's.

Their ancestors had emigrated from Thuringia to Russia and had become so Russified that Stassov, in order to give their German name a Russian tinge, nicknamed them the *Purgatzi*. However, their father, Nikolai, who in government service had reached a civil rank equal to that of a general, liked to be addressed according to the German custom, as "Mr. General," and his wife as "Mrs. General."

Most of the Purgold children were artistically endowed, and for the development of their talents were indebted to their uncle, Vladimir, who, after their father's death in 1860, replaced his brother in taking care of the family. Although he was also in government service, Vladimir was an ardent music lover, had studied voice in his youth, and was an old friend of Glinka and Dargomizhsky.

But since his musical capacity was not sufficient for him to participate in Dargomizhsky's musicales, he amused himself by staging dramatic plays, of which he himself was the author, at the Purgolds' home. The subjects of his plays were strictly "domestic" in character, as indicated by the announcement: "The action takes place in Nikolai Purgold's home." The cast was chosen from among the members of the family, and each one had to "portray himself" in such productions as *The Beginning of an End*, *Where To Find a Comedy?*, *The Arrival of the Aunt*, or *The Children's Masquerade Ball*.

Some of these performances were embellished with several musical numbers, selected and directed by Dargomizhsky, for the artistic activities of their homes were closely associated. Dargomizhsky was especially interested in Nadezhda's and Alexandra's musical development, and on his advice the girls received a thorough musical education. Neither specifically a vocal nor a piano teacher, he nevertheless helped them acquire a wide knowledge of musical literature by playing the transcriptions of orchestral works on the piano with Nadezhda, and by going through a large repertory of vocal compositions with Alexandra. This musical practice was made possible because Nadezhda had developed a remarkable ability at "reading" orchestral scores, while Alexandra had a soprano voice with an unusually wide range. Thus the two sisters became accomplished musicians in addition to being very attractive.

Not only the difference in their ages distinguished them.

Nadezhda's features were regular, and her smooth forehead above slender eyebrows was especially fine. "Look at that Greek profile," Dargomizhsky used to whisper to guests at his musicales. "What innocence and purity are expressed in her face. . . ." But she was totally unaware of her charm, as, simply dressed, she moved gracefully about the room. Though reserved, she had deep feelings, and she inspired tender respect in everyone who met her.

In contrast to her sister, Alexandra was a passionate and strong-willed young woman—it was manifested in everything about her. She had to attract and even dominate everyone's attention, or else disappointment would cloud the lively expression in her face. Her hair was carefully drawn back in a chignon, with her face framed by ringlets of her dark locks.

Although Nadezhda combed her almost black hair into two braids forming a crown on her head, Stassov used to refer to the girls as "the one with the chignon," and "the one—without."

Modeste was introduced to them when Dargomizhsky was coaching Alexandra in her part as Doña Anna in his opera *The Stone Guest*, after the Pushkin drama, which he had begun in 1868. "Like a magician pulling them out of his hat, he would produce new fragments from his opera each time we saw him," remarked Nadezhda, who was playing the orchestral part on the piano. And at a rehearsal of one of the scenes, Dargomizhsky asked Moussorgsky to sing the part of Leporello.

Nothing can be compared to the wonderful artistic atmosphere that reigned at those small gatherings, where every member was a significant talent, and brought with him his own poetic atmosphere, which exists in the nature of an artist deeply devoted to his work and inspired by his creation. Everyone brought his compositions or fragment of whatever he was working on. One would bring a new scherzo; another, a new song; the third, part of a symphony or overture; the fourth, a chorus; the fifth, an operatic ensemble or the score of an opera. How rich they were in poetry, fantasy, inspiration! Then the whole group would crowd around the grand piano, where either Balakirev or Moussorgsky would play or accompany. And immediately there were rehearsals, criticism, evaluations of merits and faults; and then the best-liked compositions were played and sung, further spurring on their inspiration.

Although Stassov said this about the Thursday meetings at Dargomizhsky's, it was also true about the "evenings" regularly held on Mondays and Fridays at Shestakova's, on Wednesdays at Balakirev's, on Saturdays at the Opochinins', and on Sundays at Stassov's. And everywhere Modeste was welcome for his enthusiastic encouragement in all their plans and activities.

Still, his reserved manner, which was ascribed to his extreme pride, made him wait for someone else to begin a conversation. He gave the impression of being a man who would talk only to those who considered this a special pleasure and even privilege, and he would never be the first to show his latest composition, but would wait to be asked.

However, he quickly became a close friend of the Purgold sisters, and when he wanted them to hear his recently written compositions, he would choose a time when he could be alone with them so that he could have their exclusive attention. But he also liked to amuse them and himself by teasing them and joking, and at Shestakova's he must have made some risqué remarks in their presence which surprised and shocked their hostess. "Oh, don't worry about it," Modeste laughed. "They are too pure, too innocent to understand."

Shestakova was surprised because she knew Moussorgsky as a man of extreme delicacy, gentility of manner, and self-control. She never saw him loose his temper, forget himself, or speak an unpleasant word to anyone. In fact, on more than one occasion, she had remarked how well he was able to control himself. "I owe this to my mother. She was a real saint," Moussorgsky said.

Not only were women susceptible to Modeste's personality—his spirit, charm, and wit; men were, too. Strangers observing him from a distance saw in him just another dandy, an immaculately dressed aristocrat with hands encased in lavender gloves. On knowing him better, however, they were completely disarmed by his shyness and timidity, by the swiftly changing expressions of his face—one moment severe and the next turning to childish wholehearted laughter, and by his speech full of contrasting changes—all testifying to a nervous nature and gentle character.

Children loved him no less than he loved them. The Stassov little girls and boys soon learned the hour of his regular afternoon visits and they would leave their games and wait to hear the doorbell ring so that they could run toward him, announcing in their gay high voices, "Moussoryanin has come, Moussoryanin has come." They knew that he had either brought them new toys or that he would join them in their games or take them to the piano, where he would improvise and tell them fascinating stories. They were drawn to him because he lacked that condescending manner which they resented in others who treated them according to their age. He called the girls "young noblewomen," and when greeting them, always kissed their hands as he would when meeting a grown woman.

His intimate knowledge of the psychology of children as well as his ability to portray a "children's world" with such mastery in many of his compositions owed everything to his pleasant amusement with the Stassov children. In the memories of his own childhood, in his gentle *nyanya*'s stories and fairy tales, and now in the games he played with the Stassov children, he found the source of that "truth" which governed the tenor of his compositions. The children's imagination became reality, their actions were directed by a singular sincerity—traits that, unfortunately, children lose with maturity. The intimate knowledge of their psychology, as well as his ability to portray "a child's world," led to *The Nursery*, his most charming contribution to musical literature. Moussorgsky's "A Children's Song" (composed in April, 1868, to a text of Lev A. Mey) was a sort of prelude to the six songs he was to compose during the following years, and which, at Stassov's suggestion, were combined into a cycle. Against the background of his own gentle poetry, Moussorgsky depicted the innocence, curiosity, and bewilderment of a child.

No wonder, then, that Modeste, more than anybody else in the Balakirev group, was curious when Dargomizhsky began his new opera, "trying to do the unheard of," as Dargomizhsky said, of writing the music to scenes from Pushkin's *The Stone Guest* just as they were, without altering a single word from the original text. (Pushkin's *Stone Guest* is a version of the Don Juan legend that is different from Mozart's. The "Stone Guest" is a statue of the Commander, whom Don Juan invites to dine.)

Dargomizhsky's example was contagious, and when Dargomizhsky, half in jest, and Cui, quite seriously, suggested to Moussorgsky that he compose an opera based on Gogol's "The Marriage," Modeste, although dismayed, accepted the challenge. He was dismayed because he knew that he was expected to solve a difficult problem—that of writing music not to verse but to Gogol's prose.

Modeste retired to Shilovo, another of Philarète's estates, and while living in an old peasant hut, he worked intensively, without a piano, on the score of his opera. He believed that his technique of writing the opera was merely a sequel to the one he had already used in his songs. He wrote to his old friend Vladimir Nikolsky:

Without preparation, you cannot make a soup. Preparing oneself to work, even though it might be Gogol's "Marriage," a most capricious thing in music, wouldn't that be the achievement of a good deed—that is, wouldn't that mean a closer approach to the most cherished aim in life?

And as if reviewing his previous compositions, he added:

Why is one always "preparing oneself"? it is about time *to do* something. The trifling little pieces [Modeste meant the songs he had already composed] were merely a preparation. If *The Marriage* is also a preparation—when, one may ask, will something finally be accomplished? To this there is only one answer —*the power of necessity*—someday it may be ready.

But he said:

It would be silly to be bashful and put on modest airs when one realizes that those "trifling little pieces" have given me a name, though only among a limited circle. These trifles have provoked a desire in persons who are rather imposing in music [Dargomizhsky and Cui] to give me an untouched (in the history course of music) problem—set everyday prose in a form of musical prose. To prove that the solution of such a problem is not easy, I offer my humble self.

He was so absorbed by the idea of re-creating human speech in music that he had trained himself to hear spoken words as a musical phrase. His aim went a step further than that of Dargomizhsky's precept: he wanted his characters not merely to speak like real people in everyday life, but to speak exactly like Gogol's characters, with their particular intonation. He wrote to Stassov:

Oh, how many sides there are to the Russian nature that art has not touched! Oh, how much! And so juicy and lovable! Only a part of it all have I re-created for my friends in musical pictures. If God will grant me longer life and strength, I will share with my people even more important things. After *Marriage* the Rubicon will be crossed. *Marriage* is a cage in which I am locked until I become tame, and then—freedom. All this is desirable, but it isn't yet there. Yet it should be there. It is terrifying. And it is terrifying because it might happen, and it might not happen because it isn't there yet.

That his feeling toward his task was not a mere pose of affectation and that he approached his task with utter humility can be seen in the following few lines in a letter he wrote to Vladimir Nikolsky:

The other day I received a most charming letter from our dear dove [this was his endearing way of referring to Shesta-

kova] but I must have a reservation about it. Speaking of my
talent, she added a word which could lead me to Olympus. I
don't understand the word—*genius*. To my way of thinking a
clever conversationalist is a good thing. I wish him well and,
as best I can, I talk with him, and if my words find a response
in his soul and his brain, I have done my work, and what hap-
pens later is "in the hands of authorities," as they say. Once,
before my departure to the country, she threw this word
["genius"] at me. I shuddered, and now she has written it, and
I broke into a sweat. I am firmly convinced that only humility
in work can guarantee independent creative ability. Why force
a man to depend on the garnishes of a full-dress uniform?"

When in the autumn Modeste returned to St. Petersburg, he was ready to show his *Marriage* to his friends. It
was given a private performance at the Purgold home with
Moussorgsky singing the leading roles. The Purgolds
were delighted, as were Borodin and Rimsky-Korsakov.
Dargomizhsky congratulated Modeste on surpassing him
in his credo, but Balakirev and Cui rejected *The Marriage*
as a mere curiosity piece.

It pained Modeste that Mili had not expressed at least a
few words of encouragement at a time when he needed
friendly support. His opera was far from being completed—
he had written only the first act, and fretted about the second and third. "I know that they *must* be good," he reas-
sured himself, and yet in the same breath he wavered, "but
I don't know whether they *can* be good."

It is true that Modeste had gradually been loosening
himself from Mili's grasp, but this was the first time that a
definite coolness had affected their relationship, and it was
not entirely Modeste's fault.

❧ *Six* ❧

~~~~~~

MILI'S was a complex personality. In addition to his remarkable leadership of his group of musicians, he had some less attractive personal characteristics which eventually alienated even his most devoted friends. He had an unusual capacity for new musical ideas, but he was too nervous, too easily irritated, and above all too impatient to bring an embryo idea to its full fruition. This was true of some of his compositions, and it was true when he imposed his ideas on his disciples, if one may so call the members of his group.

By the time Mili had finished criticizing one of their works, arbitrarily cutting whole fragments here and adding some of his own there, the composition had completely lost its author's identity, and become "Mili's, Mili's, Mili's," as Borodin remarked. He wanted each one of his pupils to be created in his own image, and tried this with every one of them; not one of them survived it.

Modeste probably put up with Mili's dictatorial manner much longer than anybody else in his group. But with

Modeste, Mili carried it further than usual, objecting to his style of life and his friends. Mili may have claimed that his concern was motivated purely by his interest in Moussorgsky's progress in music, but it did not appear that way to Modeste: he, like the others, saw the same despotic desire to control his whole being.

Mili disapproved of the Shilovskys and Modeste's long visits with them, he sharply criticized Modeste's student friends in Moscow, he was annoyed by Modeste's living in the *Commune*, and he was very much opposed to his staying with the Opochinins. Mili expressed his views freely, never sparing Modeste's feelings, and yet Modeste apparently used the self-control so much admired by Shestakova and still remained his devoted younger friend.

Mili was scornful of Modeste's wasting time on composing "trifles"—"little songs"—when he expected from him a major orchestral work. But when Modeste showed him the first version of *Witches*, Mili proceeded to blue-pencil the whole score; discouraged, Modeste spent almost three years shaping and reshaping the composition in his mind before achieving the final version in which he would not alter a single bar. While haunted by the idea of making a more powerful symphonic work of *Witches*, he was influenced decisively after reading *Witchcraft and Mysterious Phenomena of Modern Times* by Matvei Khotinsky, published in St. Petersburg in 1866.

On June 23, 1867, St. John's Eve, he completed the composition on which he had been working for three weeks up to the very last night. He had substituted the title *Night on Bald Mountain* for *Witches*, and it was a musical picture with the following program: 1) Assembly of Witches, Their Chatter and Gossip; 2) Satan's Cortege; 3) Unholy Glorification of Satan; and 4) Witches' Sabbat.

Two weeks later, in a letter to Rimsky-Korsakov (July 5, 1867), Modeste said: "There is a book, *Witchcraft*, by Matvei Khotinsky, containing a very graphic description of a witches' sabbat provided by the testimony of a woman on trial, who was accused of being a witch, and had confessed to the court love pranks with Satan himself. The poor lunatic was burnt—this occurred in the sixteenth century. From this description I took my conception of the sabbat." Moussorgsky was referring to the following in Khotinsky's book:

In 1578 Jeanne Hervilliers of Verberie near Compiègne, whose mother was burned for witchcraft, was held for investigation for the same crime. Without any torture this woman confessed that when yet an infant, she had been committed by her mother to the evil spirit, with whom she had sexual relations since the age of twelve. For thirty years the spirit had visited her, even on her nuptial bed, without arousing the suspicions of her husband. She confessed to committing several murders and to corrupting persons, and although such depositions had no proofs and were obviously invented, the judges of Ribemont sentenced her to be burned at the stake. It is remarkable that this unfortunate one should want to die so quickly that she did not consent to appeal her sentence, although there was hope that the sentence could be commuted.

In Khotinsky's book Sabbats are described in the following paragraphs:

Sabbats, or festivities of the evil spirit, where sorcerers and witches gathered, usually took place on the heights of isolated mountains, such as Brocken or Brocksberg in Germany, Blokula in Sweden, and Bald Mountain near Kiev. More women than men attended these gatherings, and witches were more honored by the Devil. . . . He who smeared himself with a special ointment fell into a deep sleep. He then saw the Devil in the form of a black goat, seated on a stone or rotting tree stump. . . .

The goat was worshiped in the most vile way, which we would not dare to describe here in Russian, using the original Latin instead. . . .

Dances started in which men and women danced with each other, and also with the demons who made up the retinue of the Devil. The majority of these had the appearance of wolves, goats, toads, and all sorts of reptiles. They were at once transformed into handsome young men, and became partners of the women who came to the Sabbat. They usually danced back to back. At this point unspeakably vile things occurred. . . .

Sabbats could occur any night and differed only in the character of the sins and vile things that took place there. However, they usually took place on Fridays, the eve before Saturday, and the main annual Sabbat was celebrated on St. John's Eve. . . . [In Russia] at night the witches, hair falling over their shoulders, mount brooms, oven forks, spades, besoms, or whisk-brooms, and fly up the chimneys to the Sabbat on Bald Mountain or the Devil's Lode, where the sorcerers and demons and sometimes Baba-Yaga assemble. But in general the whole process of the departure to the Sabbat and what takes place there is very similar to that in Western Europe, described above.

Modeste dedicated the composition to Mili, and in a letter accompanying the score he wrote that the piece was "truly *Christian*—a composition presenting a true picture of folk imagination, born in the Russian fields and nourished by Russian bread, a piece devoid of all somber German philosophy and routine, and which need not be vaguely entitled 'In A minor' or 'In D major.' "

For three months Modeste anxiously awaited Mili's reaction, but when he finally received Mili's letter, it plunged him from the heights of exhilaration—his "triumph"—into a deep depression. "This was a composer's dumps, although it is shameful to confess," Modeste wrote Mili after he had recovered from his gloom, "but it is true that that was a composer's *acidification* caused by your evasive response to my *Witches*. I consider, I consider, and I will continue to consider this piece as good, particularly because in it, after several 'trifles,' for the first time I independently approached a large work."

Mili seldom if ever changed his first impressions, and he was still looking forward to a more important composition from Modeste. Since Anton Rubinstein had resigned from the Russian Musical Society and Mili had been appointed his successor—which thus made him virtually a dictator of the musical life in St. Petersburg—Mili needed major works from the "Mighty Five" to popularize their cause of creating a national music.

He could have presented Modeste's composition, even if it did not meet with his approval, but he did not, and Modeste saw less of him than he did of Dargomizhsky. Mili was no longer as welcome at the Dargomizhsky Thursdays as he once had been. Rimsky-Korsakov, whom Mili had been determined to mold in his own fashion while Nikolai was a mere boy, was drawing away from Mili now that he had matured, and he and Modeste were steadily becoming closer friends. Mili took this as a personal affront from his two youngest disciples and as a sign of losing control over his own creation, the "Mighty Five"—a loss that might shake to its foundation his whole *raison d'être*.

It hurt Mili that this first break in their relationship came at a time when he was at last in a position to present the new works of his group of young composers. For his programs he needed symphonic music, not operas, and Dargomizhsky's sudden influence was ill-timed, as far as Mili was concerned. He disapproved of Rimsky-Korsakov's enthusiasm for *Antar*, as a subject for his symphony, a novel by the Polish author Sienkovsky, because it was Polish, and not Russian, although he himself had originally suggested the work. And as for Modeste's *Marriage*, he thought it "plain madness." Mili was even skeptical about Dargomizhsky's *Stone Guest*. "All very clever, I'm sure," he said to Stassov. "It probably has a lot of good things in it, but he will miss the point."

Mili's feelings and opinions, however, were no longer seriously considered, for the meetings at Dargomizhsky's were preoccupied with *The Stone Guest* on which—ever since his health had taken a turn for the worse during the autumn of 1868 (he suffered from a heart aneurysm)—he had worked hastily, in order to complete the opera before he died.

Dargomizhsky died in the early morning of January 5, 1869, only a few hours after Mili had at last conducted a symphony of his choice—Borodin's First Symphony. "At last" because without Mili's constant prodding of the composer, Borodin's symphony would have never gone beyond separate sketches; and "at last" because Borodin's symphony was in Mili's eyes an important major contribution to the "Mighty Five's" cause.

By that time Modeste's formerly close friendship with Mili had come to an end. In October of 1868, at one of the evenings at Shestakova's, Nikolsky suggested Pushkin's *Boris Godunov* as the subject for an opera. And Modeste Moussorgsky, as if he had been just waiting for *Boris*, dropped all his plans for other compositions, including the unfinished *Marriage*, and plunged into the new project. This was the last straw for Mili.

The pianist is Nadezhda Purgold, the singer Alexandra Purgold; Moussorgsky is standing next to the piano. Seated (left to right) are Rimsky-Korsakov, Stassov, Borodin, and Ludmilla Shestakova; standing (left to right) are Balakirev and Cui

Philarète (left), Moussorgsky's older brother, and Modeste

Moussorgsky in Military Uniform

Moussorgsky in a formal pose

Portrait of Rimsky-Korsakov by Ilya Repin

Portrait of Cui by Ilya Repin

Balakirev

Portrait of Stassov by Ilya Repin

Borodin

Dargomizhsky

A caricature of "The Mighty Five," drawn in pastels by Makovsky, when the group refused to give a private performance of Dargomizhky's *The Stone Guest* for Turgenyev, the Russian novelist, who had offended it with remarks about Glinka and Balakirev in his novel *On the Eve*.

From left to right: Cui; Balakirev, with baton in hand; Stassov, dressed in national Russian costume, blowing the horn of fame and beating a drum; Victor Hartmann, architect and artist, whose exhibition of pictures inspired Moussorgsky's *Pictures at an Exhibition*, sitting on Stassov's shoulder; and Borodin.

In front: Rimsky-Korsakov as a crab, with the two Purgold girls as little lap dogs; Moussorgsky leading the whole parade as an arrogant rooster.

The hardly visible head at the right is that of Alexander Serov, looking like Zeus shooting arrows.

❧ *Seven* ❧

LUDMILLA SHESTAKOVA presented Modeste with a vol-
ume of Pushkin's works that included the dramatic
play *Boris Godunov*, Stassov rummaged in the li-
braries for documentary information on that period in Russian history, and Vladimir Nikolsky, who was a professor
of Russian history at the Imperial College of Jurisprudence
in St. Petersburg, supplied the additional material, while
Moussorgsky was, as he said, "boiling with *Boris*."

Sometimes one of the characters of the opera would keep
him awake for two consecutive nights, he related, but he
enjoyed it. "I love this, I love to compose in this way. I live
in *Boris*. I identify myself with *Boris*." Moussorgsky
meant with every character in the opera.

As a preliminary work, with Stassov's help, he made a
thorough study of the Russian language of Boris Godunov's era. As in his *Marriage* he had tried to have the characters speak in Gogol's language, so now he was going to
"express in musical sound" the Russian language as it had
been spoken in the seventeenth century. "One has to restore
the original vitality to our mutilated language," he com-

mented. "The present Russian language resembles a man who is forced to wear shoes with too high a heel and that are much too narrow, crippling his toes. At least for a while he should be wearing comfortable *bast* shoes, like those worn by our peasants."

He followed the principles already established by the "Mighty Five": "the vocal music should match the meaning of the words; for each phrase of the text there should be a sound that corresponds to it. It is from the text's meaning that the musical ideas should be derived, since it is the function of the sounds to complete the significance of the words."

"My music," Modeste told Shestakova, "must reproduce the people's language even in the most insignificant nuances. Thus, the sounds of words, which represent an exterior manifestation of the thoughts and emotions, must, without any exaggeration or violence, become genuine and authentic but highly artistic." In his choice of a text, therefore, he had to look for "art" in the text itself in order to create a composition that would be both poetic and dramatic.

While Moussorgsky admitted that "the subject had been taken from the dramatic version of the same name by Pushkin," his interpretation of the subject radically differed from the poet's, while "preserving some part of his verses." In Moussorgsky's opera it was not Boris Godunov who was to be the hero of the drama but the Russian people; and the tragedy was to be not Boris' personal drama but again that of the Russian people. "I imagine the people as a great personality inspired by a great idea," Moussorgsky maintained.

He also followed the principles of the Balakirev group in the structure of the opera which, rejecting the progressive development of a "conflict," as it was known on the Western European stage, insisted that the real essence of the opera lies in the *idea* of the represented work. Whether this idea was expressed in series of pictures (dramatic or not in themselves) was unimportant, as long as the presentation of the whole was vivid and vital. His opera in its first version consisted of seven scenes: Prologue; the Coronation of Boris; Pimen's Cell; At an Inn Near the Lithuanian Border; the Czar's Residence in the Kremlin; In front of the Cathedral of Basil the Blessed; and Boris' Death.

"I have never realized," Moussorgsky said, "how much tranquillity is necessary for the creation of a serious work, and that it is impossible to concentrate unless one locks oneself in a small box, so to speak, from which one can observe the world and see the people as they really are."

He found this "small box" at the Opochinins', whose hospitality he had accepted when he was without government employment, and where he remained after Alexander Opochinin had procured for him a post at the Department of Forests of the Crown Lands. Nadezhda Opochinina knew how to provide Modeste with an atmosphere in which he could forget his daily drudgery at the office.

But somehow he was bashful at having his friends visit him there. "Nadezhda Petrovna [Opochinina] left word she was not at home," he would later apologize to whoever called on him there, "because she was not dressed—this is the arrangement she has established: until two o'clock in the afternoon she is not at home to visitors."

He purposely kept away from Mili, who had already

made some scathing remarks about Modeste's new work, but he needed encouragement, and each time he completed part or all of a scene, he would come out of his lair, as he said, to see the Purgold sisters, to "try it out." And indeed he found at the Purgolds' a most appreciative audience, and in the two sisters enthusiastic collaborators in the initial private performances at their home. For some time Nadezhda Purgold, observing closely her sister's changing moods and behavior, had come to the conclusion that Alexandra was in love with Modeste. She could easily understand her: she herself found him so attractive, his aristocratic manners and sense of humor so engaging, that with her impulsive response to his visits, although unwittingly, she made Alexandra jealous.

Modeste's attitude toward them, on the other hand, was one of gentle and thoughtful affection that differed only slightly and innocently in his behavior toward each of them. He was more serious in his discussions with Nadezhda than with Alexandra with whom he liked to joke, to "clown," Nadezhda thought. And this irritated Alexandra, made her moody, and even made her go to such extremes as insisting that he "hated" her. The sisters did not take seriously Moussorgsky's relationship with "that woman," as Nadezhda called Opochinina. Obviously, they did not regard it as any different from the friendship he had with them. Except for the dedication of some of his compositions to Opochinina, he kept his feelings toward her entirely to himself.

In 1859, shortly after meeting Opochinina he had dedicated to her one of his earliest works, Impromptu Passionné, inspired by one of the most ardent love scenes in

Alexander Herzen's novel *Who Is to Blame?* He also dedicated to her one of his first songs, "If Only I Could Have Met Thee Once Again!", written in August, 1863, in the form of a ballad on a text by V. Kourochkin. Although it cannot be ascribed to any particular event, except for Moussorgsky's living in the country at Volok away from Nadezhda, the twice-repeated phrase "If only I could meet thee once again!" signifies regret for an unattainable dream of love.

Eight months later, in April, 1864, he dedicated to her "The Night," a fantasy for voice with piano accompaniment set to a text by Pushkin. And while living at her home in St. Petersburg he had also composed "Desire," a ballade for voice and piano accompaniment. He marked the vocal score with, "the night of April 15–16, 1866, completed at 2 A.M." He used a text of Henrich Heine—*"Ich wolte meine Schmerzen ergössen"* ("I fain would pour forth all my sorrow")—and in dedicating it to Opochinina, he wrote on the score, "In memory of her verdict of me." This sentence and the specifically marked hour indicate his deep feeling for Nadezhda.

Otherwise Modeste had never given even a hint to the "form" of his love for Opochinina. He left the curious to speculate, and indeed their conjectures were always based on the same fact—the discrepancy in the ages of the two, which seemed to commentators a natural barrier to the fulfillment of their love. Yet, many examples in the history of great men and women prove that such an obstacle need not even be considered by two lovers.

Alexandra Purgold, puzzled by Moussorgsky's attitude toward herself and her sister, was often irritated by his discreetly evading the issue, as it seemed to her. She wished to hear the words she had been hoping for, but Modeste never uttered them.

After Dargomizhsky's death the Purgolds' home had become the center of the "Mighty Five's" musicales. While Moussorgsky's sincere and warm friendship with the two sisters was growing closer through his constant "tryouts" of the score of *Boris*, Rimsky-Korsakov's and Nadezhda's relationship had developed into a true romance. Because of the frequent visits of the two young composers, the Purgolds had dispensed with the *jour fixe* and held their musicales on any day during the week. They were often joined by Stassov, Shestakova, Borodin, and occasionally by Cui, but not by Balakirev, who had his own troubles.

In directing the Russian Musical Society concerts, he had difficulties both with the Board of Directors and with the men in the orchestra. Accustomed to the programs of his predecessor—Anton Rubinstein—they were expecting a similar choice from Balakirev, that is, predominantly works by German composers. But Mili had no patience with their opinions and desires. Since most of the members of the Board of Directors owed their position in the organization to their social and financial status rather than to their competence in musical matters, it required diplomacy to solve the problems in which they had a decisive voice. Entirely absorbed in the value of the works from a musician's point of view, Mili was incapable of adjusting himself to the situation, and only rarely was he willing to compromise by conducting Beethoven's "Eroica," Mozart's Requiem, and even Wagner's Overture to *Meistersinger*, which he hated.

He failed to please them and the critics, who wrote in

their reviews that "even a second-rate musician from a vaudeville orchestra could have done better."

If his performances of these works fell short of Mili's usual high standards, it was undoubtedly because of his strained relationship with the men of the orchestra. Mili, a poor psychologist, relied entirely on his knowledge and capacity to communicate his interpretation of a work to the orchestra. But the means he employed failed to achieve this aim. Whether or not it ever occurred to him, he certainly disregarded the fact that an orchestra is a capricious body of men, each of whom has his own opinions, desires, and ambitions, and who, if not treated diplomatically, would fail even the best conductor.

During his close friendship with Ulibishev, who wrote an extensive biography of Mozart, Mili must have heard that when young Wolfgang complained to his father about the insubordinate behavior of his orchestra, Leopold Mozart advised him, "You must flatter them, then you'll succeed in winning them and getting the results you desire." Such a procedure was sheer nonsense as far as Mili was concerned. He didn't even believe in encouraging them. His dictatorial manner only provoked antagonism from his men, who were used to Rubinstein's "German and *klassisch* ways," a manner that Mili assumed only when he wanted to emphasize his utter contempt for Germans. He referred to them as *Die Hasenfüsse*, the cowards, completely forgetting that he was speaking to some *Hasenfüsse* in his orchestra.

Ever since he had accepted the appointment as their leader in the autumn of 1867, Mili surprised them by addressing them in Russian. "What kind of language is this to talk music in?" grumbled the musicians, who were predominately German. And Mili's Russian was often very plain Russian; he cursed them in words that are well-known though they have never been printed in any dictionary. The musicians resented his behavior, and many of them resigned—something that in no way affected Mili's customary attitude.

He was even less popular with the Grand Duchess Elena Pavlovna, who, in Mili's opinion, acted as if she owned the Russian Musical Society. Mili was well aware that by appointing him as leader of the Society and by inviting a few men who were connected with the Free Music School, she had hoped to be able not only to influence and direct, but actually to control the stubborn band of "Balakirevs."

Mili could not care less for her opinions, and although always cordial to her, he kept his distance and his independence. Flattered by Anton Rubinstein's seeking her help and guidance (there was a rumor, well or ill founded, that their mutual ecstasy was not limited to the area of German classical sounds), she considered Mili uncouth, in need of being "Westernized" so that she could "polish him up." She had even hinted at a journey abroad for this purpose, but Mili treated it as mere rumor. Very much annoyed, Her Royal Highness saw to it that Mili was not re-engaged for the following season. Thus, after two years of comparatively safe existence, he was left with the Free Music School, which had no money, and the prospect of going back to giving piano lessons in order to earn his living.

While the "Mighty Five," and Moussorgsky especially, wholeheartedly endorsed Mili's stand vis-à-vis the Board of Directors of the Russian Musical Society, the orchestra, and the Grand Duchess, and sympathized with his financial plight, they did not welcome the change in his attitude toward them.

Mili had originally suggested to Borodin that he compose an opera based on *The Maid of Pskov*, which Borodin declined to do since he preferred *Prince Igor*, which Stassov had suggested; Modeste, in turn, urged Rimsky-Korsakov to accept Mili's original suggestion. Mili did not like his ideas to be handled in this way. Already embittered by his situation, he no longer showed any interest in his former disciples' work on operas. "An evening with Mili used to be pleasant, now an evening without Mili is even more pleasant," was the consensus at the Purgolds' meetings.

Having studied historical documents for *Boris Godunov*, Modeste was well equipped to furnish Rimsky-Korsakov's libretto with the necessary data on the epoch of Ivan the Terrible, the period in Russian history to which *The Maid of Pskov* belonged. But this was not Modeste's sole preoccupation. He carefully went over his score and only then, urged by his friends, did he summon courage to take his *Boris* to Stepan Gedeonov, the Director of the Imperial Theatres, which included the Maryinsky Theatre. He was told that there were no plans for producing new operas, but that if there were any changes in the following season's repertory, he would be notified.

Modeste was too certain of his opera's qualities to doubt Gedeonov's sincerity or to suspect a prejudice because he was a member of the "Mighty Five," against whom continuous intrigues were being plotted by the conservative musicians in St. Petersburg. Ever since the appearance of the Balakirev group in the musical life of St. Petersburg, the musicians and the audiences were split into two warring camps—each with its mouthpiece in the press and its music critics who spared no paper or ink in writing abusive articles against each other, some so slanderous that the authors had to be taken to court.

Modeste's devotion to the cause of the "Mighty Five" never wavered, and was never affected by either Mili's criticisms of his work or Cui's condescending attitude. Three years earlier, in 1867, when Modeste had been experimenting with "humor in music," he had composed "The Seminarist," for basso or baritone with piano accompaniment, in which he ridiculed the classicists. Because it would not pass the Russian censorship, he had given the score to the Purgold sisters, who were spending the summer of 1870 in Germany, to try to get it published there. Spurred on by the favorable reaction of his friends to "The Seminarist," Modeste, enrolled by Stassov into general polemic with the adversaries of the "Mighty Five," now composed another satirical piece, "The Puppet Show," mocking their antagonists, headed by the Grand Duchess Elena Pavlovna, Modeste's longtime *bête noire*.

"The Puppet Show" was undiplomatic and ill-timed as far as the chances for acceptance of *Boris* at an Imperial Theatre were concerned. If Glinka's opera *A Life for the Tsar* was highly patriotic, as its title indicated, the subject of Moussorgsky's opera was "subversive," in government authorities' parlance. It was based on Pushkin's work, which for years had been barred not only from theatrical production but also from publication. Thus, Moussorgsky's latest satire could hardly have served him as a "letter of recommendation" to Gedeonov, whose views were far from liberal.

In February, 1871, four months after Moussorgsky had left his score with the Board of Directors of the Maryinsky Theatre, *Boris* was rejected. "It was examined by a committee consisting of Eduard Napravnik, the Opera conductor, Louis Maurer, the Inspector of Music, Eduard Betz, the orchestra conductor of a German theatre, Karl Klammrodt and Voyacek, opera conductors, and Gedeonov. Except for Gedeonov, who was Russian, the others were Czech, French, and German, and could not have been expected to fathom Moussorgsky's "drama of the Russian people."

They based their rejection on the absence of a major feminine role, and on some minor difficulties of perform-ance. Everybody expected Moussorgsky to be indignant, even enraged. Instead, he quietly listened to Stassov's and Nikolsky's advice of adding to the score a love scene and an enlarged *prima donna.* He revised the first version, added two scenes which became known as the "Polish act," and transferred the scene "near Kromy," which was the next to last, to the very end of the opera. By reversing the order of the two last scenes, thus following Boris' death scene with the one in which the *yurodivyi* prophesies the "Troubled Times" confronting Russia, Moussorgsky emphasized the "drama of the Russian people," the opera's main theme. But this version was also rejected by the Board of Directors, after six months of deliberation.

Not in the least discouraged, Vladimir Purgold—the sis-ters' uncle, who was an influential personage in govern-ment, social, and musical circles—had organized a private performance of the second version of *Boris* with the participation of the best-known singers in the capital. Eventually, this led to the production at the Maryinsky Theatre of three scenes. Modeste was so eager to have *Boris* produced that even this piecemeal presentation sent him into raptures. "Champagne was drunk with toasts for a speedy performance of the entire *Boris*," Rimsky-Korsakov related after an all-night celebration of their victory.

❧ *Eight* ❧

IN 1871 Rimsky-Korsakov was offered the post of Professor of Composition, Orchestration, and Conducting in the orchestra classes at the St. Petersburg Conservatory. This proposition had stirred even Balakirev, who showed little interest in his former disciples' musical activities, for he was gratified in seeing "one of his own men" accepted in the "enemy camp." And Cui echoed Mili's satisfaction in one of his articles saying, "It is particularly significant, this invitation to one of the representatives of the contemporary movement of young Russian composers." They urged Rimsky-Korsakov to accept it, despite his own admission that he was not equipped to *teach* composition and that he would have to learn theoretical subjects, as taught at the conservatory, from his own pupils. But his final decision was directed by his personal life. He was going to marry Nadezhda Purgold, and he had hoped to leave the naval service to devote himself entirely to music. But before he could realize these plans, he decided to combine the two professions.

For years he had been living by himself in a small furnished room, spending most of the time at the home of his brother, Voin. In the fall of 1871 Voin had gone to Italy for his health, their mother was away on a long visit in Moscow, and Rimsky-Korsakov felt lonely. Modeste, his closest friend, sympathized with him, and the two agreed to solve the problem by sharing a furnished room in a boarding house. This was the only instance in the history of music in which two composers lived together in such close quarters, each working on his own compositions.

The general conception of musicians as men of temperamental idiosyncracies and petty jealousies would make this kind of arrangement seem impossible, and yet, despite their differences as human beings, they did not get in each other's way and actually even benefited by this close contact. Modeste's advice improved Rimsky-Korsakov's recitative and declamatory skill, while Rimsky-Korsakov restrained Modsete's frequent indulgence in, what seemed to him, exaggerated expressions of his "bizarre originality," and helped to polish his rough harmonization and occasionally illogical constructions in his scores, trying to make Modeste's compositions more palatable to the tastes of the time.

They found no difficulty in scheduling their daily work so as not to disturb each other. During the afternoons Modeste was at his office, and he often dined and spent entire evenings at the Opochinins', where, when he felt like it, he could work. And twice a week Rimsky-Korsakov was away, teaching at the conservatory. Thus, there were only occasional mornings when each one might need the piano. But they did not mind, and in fact, although Modeste was working on his score of *Boris*, he had learned Rimsky-Kor-sakov's *Maid of Pskov* so well that he later performed the entire opera from memory for their friends.

Not all of their mornings were occupied exclusively with their work. Stassov, on the way to his office at the Public Library, often breakfasted with them; Borodin would join them, and the two roommates showed their guests the progress of their daily work, playing and singing excerpts from their operas. When one of them had to leave to attend to more prosaic duties, the others remained until his return. Even Cui, out of pure curiosity, interrupted his sedate life at home to partake of these musical conferences.

Sometimes they walked the short distance to Borodin's apartment to hear his Second Symphony, which he had begun after his discouragement with the slow progress of his *Prince Igor*. Stassov would scold Borodin for such an early acknowledgment of defeat in the face of some operatic problems, while Borodin protested that none of the material already written was being wasted, since he was using it in his symphony. Both Rimsky-Korsakov and Modeste agreed with Stassov and urged Borodin to continue his opera in preference to a symphonic work, and still discussing the predominant values of operas, they would return home, often forgetting that the day was nearing its end.

But the happy rooming together was terminated when on July 12, 1872, Rimsky-Korsakov married Nadezhda Purgold. Modeste was his best man. Four months later, in November, Alexandra Purgold married Nicholas Mollas, a government official and an amateur landscape painter, and again Modeste served as best man. It seemed as if Modeste was destined to remain merely a witness to happiness. He once told Shestakova that if she heard that he had committed suicide, it would simply mean that he had married.

Again Modeste was left alone and more lonely than ever, for he saw the world of his musical friends crumbling. The marriage of the two Purgold sisters put an end to the home of that "musical world." While Rimsky-Korsakov was still on his honeymoon, Modeste was predicting that with his new professorial post at the Conservatory, and consequently inevitable connections with the "conservatives," Rimsky-Korsakov would eventually be lost to the "Mighty Five" cause.

As a composer, Cui had never shown in his songs or operas any ideological influence, nor did he strive to break new paths for future Russian music. His main and important contribution to the "Mighty Five" cause lay in his literary popularization of their ideas. Since 1864, his articles and musical criticisms had appeared in St. Petersburg newspapers and periodicals. He signed them with three little stars in the form of a triangle, the insignia he wore on his epaulettes as a lieutenant in the Russian Army.

His style was clear, but the bitter sarcasm in which he sometimes indulged made more enemies than friends for him. Although devoted to his friends' cause, he was just as critical of some of their works—in fact, in his ardor for criticism Cui the critic criticized Cui the composer. When, after several successful productions of his opera *Ratcliff*, a singer missed his cue and thus upset the eighth performance and Cui heard booing in the audience, he lost his temper; in his column the next day he asked the St. Petersburg public to refrain from attending future performances of his opera whenever they were announced.

Cui lived a firmly established life in which no conceivable changes could have occurred. He taught at the Military Academy, and within the four walls of his happy home with his family he composed, adding every summer another act to his opera *Angelo* on a medieval subject that did not interest Modeste.

When Borodin at his first meeting with the Balakirev group said that he was only a Sunday composer who strove to remain obscure, he had never said a truer word about himself. Lazy—it took him seventeen years to complete his *Prince Igor*—and lacking any ambition, he was content to live in the most disorderly fashion, personally and professionally.

Even those who did not expect typical German *Ordnung* would have been startled at the sight of Borodin's apartment. But it had a simple explanation. The apartment had been allotted to Borodin by the Academy of Medicine, where he was lecturing as a professor of chemistry. The living quarters were spacious—there was plenty of room for everybody, so it was said. In addition to Borodin, his wife, and two adopted daughters, it served as *pied-à-terre* for their friends and relatives, for homeless students, and for those visitors from the country who preferred Borodin's rent-free abode to any other domicile.

To accommodate themselves, they moved the furniture in bedrooms, sitting rooms, and dining room at will, paying little attention to the chosen pieces, since they were all "government property," which traditionally did not require any particular care. Curtains and rugs were lying about the rooms awaiting their long-overdue placement, and a second piano intended for the living room remained in the entrance hall in everybody's way, awaiting its own location that was occupied "temporarily" by sofas, which had been turned into unmade beds by the overnight guests. "The samovar never leaves the table," the visitors informed each other, indicating that tea and a customary supply of food welcomed everybody to lively discussions on the arts and politics, occasionally interspersed with local gossip.

If not in Moscow escaping the St. Petersburg climate which was bad for her health, Ekaterina, Borodin's wife, incessantly smoking and constantly complaining, held court in her bedroom with a group of her relatives and friends. Regardless of the basis for her fears, she was afraid of typhoid and cholera, of colds and stomach aches, thunderstorms and dark nights, flies, cockroaches, and burglars; in the country she was terrified by dogs, horses, cows, chickens, little boys, and muzhiks, drunk or sober. She hated Borodin's relatives and the friends of his relatives, his students, and jobless musicians, and yet she could not bear to be alone.

Borodin's arrival home from the Academy after his lectures was scarcely noticed by the disputing guests at the dining table, except by Vaska, Borodin's favorite among the large number of cats who infested the apartment. Making room for Vaska somewhere on the table amidst half empty glasses of tea and unfinished plates of food, Borodin would correct a pile of his students' homework, not in the least disturbed by the hubbub around him.

Nowhere in this "spacious" apartment could he claim privacy, not even in his study, for the visitors, who were apt to arrive at all hours of the day or night, did not mind submerging his desk with his papers and books under a pile of sweaters, jackets, and hats; and it was not unusual for his maid, if and when she was prompted to bring some order into his study, to use his sketches for songs or parts of symphony to cover jars of sour cream or line cat boxes.

"Do you compose at night when everyone is asleep, or in the morning when the head is clear, or during the day between your lectures, or in the evenings when you are particularly inspired?" Such questions embarrassed Borodin.

Despite his almost athletic constitution, Borodin constantly suffered from something. If he did not have a cold, he had boils, or toothaches that swelled one side of his face —which on his wife's insistence he treated with hot compresses—or such a stomach ache (*"locus minoris resistantiae"*) from feasting on roast goose with kasha, baked apples, and cabbage at Cui's (*"C'est si peu français"*), that he would roll on the floor. And when he was exhausted from a sleepless night spent on a couch in the living room because his bed had been occupied by one of the guests, when his head was splitting and his eyes and nose were running because of the smoke from the stoves that had not been cleaned, then, as if no other conditions could inspire him, wearing an overcoat in a cold room, he would sit down at the piano and compose.

Borodin's motto for living was clear and simple: Never do anything today that can be done tomorrow, or . . . still better, at some other time. And yet he somehow, managed to compose masterpieces, to contribute valuable papers to scientific periodicals, and to be active in promoting new laws providing for higher education for women.

His friendship with the other members of the "Mighty Five" was warm and sincere, but lacking their enthusiasm, he took no sides in their disputes and always remained merely an observer. Though Modeste's relationship with Borodin was always cordial, it was never intimate, for while Borodin composed on Russian themes, he had no definite ideology underlying his music and "could not fight to the last drop of blood." He would rather, as Modeste would say, "be drinking countless cups of tea, forgetting whether he had had lunch or dinner, or whether he had had them twice."

Balakirev, their former leader and the founder of the "Mighty Five," to whom Modeste had been attracted more than to anyone else in the group and to whom he was indebted for his introduction to the idea of a national music, was now out of sight. His belief in himself and his most cherished aim—to be carried on by his disciples—was shaken. Balakirev, a proud man, seemed neither religious nor superstitious, and yet he had shown that he was not entirely free of a belief in the supernatural. At least one example of his self-deception was mentioned by his friends. Mili claimed that he had seen a ghost at the Lyadovs' country home, and no amount of evidence and argument could convince him that the apparition was staged by his friends. Since the loss of his position at the Russian Musical Society, the loss of his authority over his disciples, and the sudden death of his father, which left his two sisters in his care and thus created further financial problems, his nervous system was so disturbed that in all earnest he turned to a fortuneteller to seek solace and advice.

When and where Mili met this fortuneteller and who she was are unknown. According to Shestakova, who saw her once when she came to her home looking for Mili, she was a beautiful young woman with large dark eyes. Shestakova thought that she was in love with Mili; others believed that she was a "real witch."

Mili sat frightened at her seances in a semi-dark room while she called forth images in a large mirror. Neither Rimsky-Korsakov, in whom Mili confided about these visits, nor Moussorgsky, who heard about them, could fathom whether Mili himself actually saw these apparitions or, merely through his medium's descriptions, was made to believe that they were the Grand Duchess Elena Pavlovna, Napravnik, or other members of the Board of Directors of the Russian Musical Society. But what was clear to them was that Mili was influenced by the fortuneteller's information about their thoughts and intentions, for he suddenly decided to raise funds for his Free Music School by giving a piano recital himself. But instead of playing in the capital, where he was known, he went to Nizhni-Novgorod, where he had been forgotten. His prediction of making a thousand rubles not only ended in fiasco as far as future plans for the Free Music School were concerned, but it was also a final blow to his self-esteem.

He returned to St. Petersburg from his "Sedan," as he called his concert in Nizhni-Novgorod, brooding and pondering on the whole meaning of life and on the place of art in human endeavor. He questioned the theory, which he himself had been preaching, that music is "an instrument of truth" and a "social force," and he decided to practice it as a sacred art, away from society. He fell under the influence of men zealous in the Russian Orthodox faith, found friends mostly among the lower clergy, and gradually conformed to their way of living.

"Don't live the way you wish to, but the way God ordains," and the dogmas of the Russian Orthodox Church slowly but persistently changed Mili and completely altered his behavior. He was constantly attending church services, following the rigid form of rituals; he developed an exaggerated faith in the power of the cross and crossed himself fervently, in addition to all prescribed occasions, whenever he passed a church, or heard thunder, sneezed, or yawned. He stopped smoking and disapproved of drinking, and became a vegetarian, although he still managed to eat fish, but only the kind that "had gone to sleep," he explained.

He gave shelter to homeless cats and dogs, but insisted on their celibacy, and often was seen rescuing his watchdog from falling prey to sin. Heavy curtains kept his apartment in semi-darkness, where the air was permeated by the smell of little oil icon lamps burning in the corner of each room. And he invariably turned the conversation to religious subjects, on which he had become an expert.

Men reserve a special etiquette for religion, whose sacred aura they dare not offend, yet Stassov, refusing to acknowledge Mili's change and more out of concern for him than from lack of tact, would plead with his old friend, "Now, how can you, an intelligent man, how can you . . . ?"

Was Mili going insane? Stassov asked himself. Perplexed by Mili's behavior, Stassov wrote to Rimsky-Korsakov and to Moussorgsky:

I must tell you that Balakirev made the saddest impression on me last night when I saw him. In appearance he looks as though nothing were changed—same voice, same face, same figure, same words—and yet, from the old nothing is left. Just imagine that from time to time there was a silence between us lasting for several minutes. I tried this way and that way, from this angle or that angle, avoiding carefully whatever might be unpleasant to him, but I saw that nothing would help. He would say a few words, and then there was silence again. When did such a thing happen? I have known him for fifteen years. No, this is another man; before me was some sort of living corpse, not the lively, energetic, restless Mili.

Ever since Mili had been critical of Moussorgsky's opera *The Marriage*, Modeste seldom saw Balakirev. In reply to Stassov he wrote:

Your lines about Mili shocked me—I was not a witness to his state of freezing. I imagine something dreadful: your words sound to me like a dirge for Mili's artistic career. Frightful! If this is real and not a passing phase, it is much too early— it is wicked *how* early! Or is it a disappointment? Well, perhaps that is what it is. But where, then, is his manliness, his courage, where is the faith in his work and in the artistic aim, which can never be achieved without a struggle? Or was the art only a means and not the aim? *Diavolo! Diavolo!* [Moussorgsky quoted from the opera *Fra Diavolo*.]

Even Borodin, the calmest and the most rational among the Five, suspected the possibility of Mili's insanity. Years earlier Balakirev had complained to Borodin of frequent headaches and an irritability that sometimes developed into hysterical fits. Mili ascribed them to an inflammation of the brain from which he had suffered during his first year in St. Petersburg. Now he had come to Borodin again seeking the name of a psychiatrist, and it was Borodin alone who knew of the intensive treatment that Mili had been undergoing.

Suppose he is not insane, Borodin thought, is this present state any better than insanity?

To everybody's surprise, Mili, entirely disregarding financial problems, announced a series of five concerts of the Free Music School. But he was no longer the man he used to be. His magnetic power in conducting the orchestra was not the same. Despite the medley of Christian mildness and of trivialities worthy of an old maid, Mili retained his past intolerance and dictatorial manner, which led to constant quarrels with his orchestra. His concerts were a failure. On April 3, 1872, he closed the program of his fourth and last concert with Moussorgsky's polonaise from the recently composed "Polish Act" in *Boris*.

A polonaise is often played as a majestic opening to a festival, and Moussorgsky's polonaise from *Boris*—one of the greatest works by a member of the "Mighty Five"— should have sounded like a fanfare to the future success of their music. Instead, it was a requiem to their once close association.

Mili Balakirev resigned from the Free Music School, and two months later he took a job as a minor clerk in the department of supplies at the Warsaw line in the Central Railway Company. The station was located on the outskirts of the city—his monthly salary amounted to eighty rubles (about forty dollars). "Today began my work at the office of the Warsaw railway. May the Lord have mercy!!!" Mili wrote in his notebook on June 6, 1872.

Mili never explained the choice of his new occupation.

Modeste mourned Mili's defeat, and five weeks later, on July 11, 1872, he wrote to Shestakova:

Our dear dove, you were the witness of our fiery creations, our struggles, our striving, and our disputes. A great deal of good has been done. Bright is the past of our musical circle—cloudy is its present, worrisome days have come. I shall not blame anyone for this, "for there is no anger in my heart," yet I cannot, no matter how I try, drive away the annoying flea that buzzes the words, "You fell apart, you fell apart"—a buzz that is like laughter, mean, wicked laughter.

But Stassov was neither ready nor willing to accept Mili's latest move, his cutting himself off from all musical activities. While still hoping that Mili would find no satisfaction in his new occupation, nevertheless worried over Balakirev's state of mind, he advised Shestakova to beg Mili to bring his manuscripts to her home for safekeeping, since they were afraid that Balakirev might suddenly burn them as Gogol had done with his. And when this suggestion had failed to show Mili their faith in his return to his true vocation, Shestakova, almost two years later, more probably as a last resort than because she was losing her patience with him, wrote to Mili:

For health or other reasons you have recently withdrawn from public life, and since you are not establishing a *permanent* musical institution, I presume you will not object if I remove *my brother's piano*, which you have, to the Conservatory.

Mili left no record of his feelings at this final humiliation caused by his retirement from music and the "Mighty

Five," except for one line in his notebook dated May 17, 1874: "Today at about ten o'clock they took from me M. I. Glinka's piano."

Of the "Mighty Five," Modeste was the only one who still had faith in what had once bound them together and made them so unselfishly happy in each other's achievements. "There will be other warriors from whose hands you cannot tear the banner." Modeste hoped; and undaunted, he held to his course. But he felt desperately alone.

"Man is a social animal," he said quoting Spinoza, and Moussorgsky was a social animal in the extreme. Since his musical friends had failed him, he turned to men in other branches of the arts, for he was the only composer of his time who showed a lively interest in literature, old and new, foreign and Russian, in painting and sculpture, as well as in history, astronomy, sociology, and science. He was acquainted with what Kant, Beneke, and Locke had to say about psychology, he knew the Baconian method of studying natural phenomena, he was eloquent in discussing Descartes' rationalistic theories in ethics and his belief in the supremacy of mind over passion, and he knew Leibnitz's treatises on immortality. Modeste was always welcome in discussions on these various subjects, since because of his personal approach to everything he read and observed, his participation made the discussions informative and stimulating. Through Stassov he met a large number of writers, painters, poets, and sculptors, and he developed close friendships with Repin, Antakolsky, and Hartmann. Ilya Repin, five years younger than Modeste, later became Russia's most famous painter. Mark Antakolsky, three years younger than Moussorgsky, had aroused public interest with his monumental sculptures and his statue "Christ before the People," which brought him European fame; and Victor Hartmann, four years older than Moussorgsky, an architect, water colorist, and designer.

In 1862 Stassov had attended an artists' masquerade ball. In the midst of a crowd of young men and women dressed up as Dantes, Mary Stuarts, Italian abbots, Turks, Spaniards, walking playing-cards, and harlequins, there was one, dressed as Baba-Yaga, the traditional witch of Russian fairy tales. As Stassov described it later, "Her red braids were streaming out behind her, a large fuzzy hat was pulled over her forehead, her feet were wrapped in coarse puttees, her bony arms stuck out of the sleeves of her robe, a sparse beard protruded from her chin, and her horrible eyes gleamed maliciously, while tusks were seen in her half-open mouth." The twenty-eight-year-old Victor Hartmann, who had just been graduated from the St. Petersburg Academy of Arts, startled the assembly in this unusual disguise.

But Stassov did not meet him until seven years later, when Hartmann caused a sensation with a design for the great gate of Kiev in a competition for a work to commemorate the day Alexander II had escaped assassination in Kiev. The son of an army doctor, Hartmann was born and educated in St. Petersburg, and after marrying a Polish woman in 1864, went abroad where he spent four years in France, Germany, Italy, and Poland. He brought back several hundred sketches he had made during his travels and it was then that Stassov introduced him to the "Mighty Five."

Moussorgsky was particularly fascinated by the sketches and drawings depicting various types of men and women in their local surroundings.

Modeste became very attached to Hartmann, "whose small body was always in motion," according to Stassov, "who always strove to create, and on whom one could always count to invent something that had never occurred to anyone else before."

Perhaps these characteristics of an *enfant terrible* had inspired Moussorgsky's song (written in 1870) "In the Corner," in his series *The Nursery*. In his own verse Moussorgsky created a dialogue between the Nurse, who was punishing a child for his "naughtiness" by making him stand in a corner of the room, and the child protesting his innocence. He dedicated the song to Victor Hartmann.

In no other circle could Modeste have found such kinship in thought and beliefs. "He alone is an artist," Antakolsky said, "who loves humanity as passionately as he loves his art, who dedicates his whole life to art for the sake of humanity. Only in such favored beings is the divine spark to be found, bright and unquenchable, and *that*, in art, is the one indispensable thing, for when the soul ceases to lend its love, the death of art begins."

Repin modestly used to remark that since he was not a musician, he could not understand why Moussorgsky was so attracted by him. He attributed it to the fact that Modeste was touched by his own admiration for Moussorgsky's musical talent, which was then far from being generally recognized. To Repin, Modeste was a nugget from Russian soil, and his looks reminded him of the giants in the Russian fairy tales. Thus, under Stassov's patronage a new friend-

ship developed among Antakolsky, Repin, and Moussorgsky, whom Stassov christened his favorite "Audacious
Troika."

During the absence of his friends from the capital—
Stassov and Antakolsky were in Moscow, Repin was in
Paris—Modeste missed their meetings, and he found com-
pensation in the letters he wrote to them. Preferring the
study in Stassov's apartment to his own "lonely" room, he
often spent many hours there, rummaging in Stassov's library or working on his score of *Boris*, which he brought
with him. He wrote to Repin:

So here is how it is, my dear glorious shaft horse. Though
the *Troika* has temporarily dispersed, still it pulls where it
should pull.

And after studying Repin's latest portrait of Stassov, which
hung on the wall of his study, Modeste, referring to this
masterpiece, added:

He actually crawls out of the canvas into the middle of the
room. What Life! What power! Painters have known for a
long time how to mix their paints and do it freely, if God has
given them sense. But our brother the musician first has to
think, then measure, and once he has taken the measure, he has
to think some more—mere childhood—a baby!

But in his letters to Stassov he continued their discussions on art, as if they had been interrupted only the day
before:

Why is it, tell me please, that when I listen to a conversation of
our young artists—painters and sculptors—I can follow the
trend of their thought and their aims, and seldom hear anything

about technique? And why, when I listen to our musical brother-
hood, do I seldom hear a live thought, but see only the school-
bench, technique, and the musical alphabet?

Is musical life so immature because it is created by the half-
witted? How many times, not purposely, but as if by chance
(sneaking from the corner) I have started such a conversation with them! Either I would be reproached, or else I was
not clear, but most probably they just could not understand.
Well, let us suppose that I am incapable of presenting my ideas
clearly—of presenting my brain, so to speak, on a tray with my
thoughts impressed on it.

And what about themselves? Why do they never mention
anything except the technique in composing? You are the only
one who understands me, and furthermore you prod me with a
sure and courageous hand.

Am I perhaps afraid of technique because I am so bad at it?
I am sure there are some who will come to my defense. For instance, I cannot bear it when the landlady, who is baking a pie,
particularly a good pie, says that a million pounds of butter,
five hundred eggs, a whole row of cabbages, one hundred fifty
and a quarter pieces of fish . . . went into the pie; for when
one hears about the "kitchen," one begins to imagine that either
the landlady or the cook is dirty, one sees the head of a capon
lying on a bench, a fish ripped open in the middle lying on another bench, and sometimes right next to it some guts peeking
from the sieve (as though cockroaches had paid a visit); and
when one imagines a greasy apron on which the cook had
blown his nose—the same apron with which he later wipes the
edge of the pie plate so that it will be good and clean. . . .
Well, the pie becomes less appetizing.

In a mature artistic creation there is always that side of
virginal purity which, if one starts touching it with dirty
hands, becomes revolting. Truly, as long as the artist does not
reject the diapers, suspenders, and leggings, the symphonic
priests who put their Bible as the Alpha and Omega of an

artistic life will reign. Their little brains feel that the Bible cannot be used in a live art where there are real people, real life—that there is no place in it for prescribed paragraphs and chapters. Well, naturally they scream "the drama, the stage, are in our way. We need space"; and to flatter themselves, they declare that the world of sound is limitless. So what could there be in the world of sound?

Why Antakolsky's "Jaroslav" and Repin's "Boatmen" are so alive, so alive that when one sees them one feels like saying, "Well, it is exactly what I had expected to see." Why is it that everything that is written in our contemporary music (in spite of some with excellent qualities) does not live like that? Please explain this to me. But put aside the limits of art. What does it matter whether some great minds did not reach the heights and others who thought about it a great deal finally did? Where, then, is the borderline? Sounds cannot be a chisel or a brush; this even children must know.

If Modeste Moussorgsky's views on art were not eloquently expressed for some people, Leo Tolstoy's essay *What Is Art?*—showing a striking similarity in their views —states the essential argument more clearly. Tolstoy and Moussorgsky did not know each other, but both were undoubtedly influenced by the writings of Nikolai Dobrolyubov and Nikolai Chernyshevsky, two champions of artistic realism, as was almost the entire Russian intelligentsia.

At the age of seventy Tolstoy predicted that "the artist of the future will be free of all perversions of technical camouflage concealing the absence of subject matter," and as if he were paraphrasing Antakolsky's statement, Tolstoy added, "and who, not being a professional artist, and receiving no payment for his activity, will produce art only when he feels compelled to do so by an irresistible inner impulse."

Did Tolstoy not know that such an artist had died in his own country almost two decades earlier?

"Pull, shaft horse, pull without fatigue," Modeste wrote to Repin:

And I, as the side horse, am also pulling somewhere so that there will be no trouble for our troika on the road. I am afraid of the whip. . . . And I feel in which direction I should push, and I carry and pull my burden. . . . This is what it is: I want to portray people; when I sleep, I see them in my dreams, and when I drink, they appear before me as a whole—real, without any paint or tinsel. Then if I succeed, I will be grateful, and if not, I will be sad. But you will not get the people out of my mind. Oh no, do not jest. You will not.

Modeste was referring to the subject of his next opera.

❧ *Nine* ❧

THE early years (1682–1689) of the reign of Peter the Great had suffered from internal struggle and from the court intrigue incited by the young Czar's European innovations. The conspiracies between the two families of Prince Narashkin and Prince Myloslavsky, the religious feud between the fantatical Old Believers and the new reformers, and the uprisings led by Prince Ivan Khovansky, who schemed to marry his son, Andrei, to one of the Princesses and to become himself the Czar—this was the dramatic period in the history of Russia which Stassov brought to Modeste's attention. Young Peter's scornful reference to his adversaries' "behavior" as mere *"Khovanshchina"*—Prince Khovansky and his son were sent to the gallows—was a perfect title for Moussorgsky's opera.

Modeste's interest in the subject was aroused by the story of the common people who had suffered during those gloomy years. He saw the struggle between the old and the new Russia at the time of Peter the Great analogous to the struggle in his own epoch. As in his *Boris* the people were to be the heros of the opera. He wrote to Stassov:

And what if Moussoryanin [Moussorgsky] strikes at Mother Russia! It is not the first time that I have dug into the black earth, and not in fertilized earth, but directly into the raw; I long not to just become acquainted with the people, but to become intimate with them, like brothers. It is terrifying! . . . But it is good!

And Modeste asked for Stassov's and Nikolsky's help in his research in all annals, memoirs, and history books that treated with that period. He continued his letter to Stassov:

What then? Why was a Russian fooled by heresy? Do I not know the answer? Do I not know where the force is hidden, where the truth lies? . . .

The black earth force will show itself when you dig to the bottom, and to dig the earth one should have a special kind of tool. And did they not dig Mother Russia at the end of the seventeenth century with such a tool that at first she did not understand what they were digging with and began to expire. And then she accepted it, the dear one, all sorts of privy councilors, and they did not give her, the dear suffering one, a chance to come to herself and think: "Where are you shoving?" The ignorant and the confused were executed. Power! . . . Strength! . . . And prison still exists and the police is the same. Only the times are different. The privy councilors still do not allow the black earth to breathe.

To put the past into the present—this is my task. "We have progressed?" You are lying—we are still where we were. On paper, in books, we have progressed, but we are still where we were. As long as the people cannot examine with their own eyes what is being done to them, we shall remain where we were. All sorts of public benefactors are ready to gain great honors and to record them in documents, but the people are groaning, and so as not to groan, they drink, and then groan all the more. "We are still where we were!"

Although Moussorgsky had not even begun to work on his score he had already dedicated the future opera to Stassov. "To me it does not matter that there is no precedent for dedicating works that do not yet exist," he wrote to Stassov. "I want to look forward, not backward." And he said that he still remembered the time when he "lived in *Boris*," "when he boiled in *Boris*," and that now he was going to "boil" in this new work. "How many rich impressions, how many new lands to discover and explore. . . . Glorious!" He already savored the research into which he was plunging with his characteristic enthusiasm.

But this time it was different. He was not living at the Opochinins', where, after his daily office work, he had found peace and comfort provided by Nadezhda Opochinina. He was still living in the room he had shared with Rimsky-Korsakov. Modeste not only hated living alone, he was afraid of it. He was afraid of being alone when he was seized with an attack of his illness.

He was fortunate at that time to meet Count Arseny Golenishchev-Kutusov, a distant relative. The twenty-five-year-old Kutusov was a poet who had recently made his debut in the literary field and was living in the same boarding house as Modeste. Like Modeste, Kutusov came from an impoverished noble family, but instead of looking for employment, he preferred to spend his time on the estates of his more fortunate relatives or in St. Petersburg, where he led a Bohemian life.

He had even ignored the government's appointment of him in the service of the Governor of the Caucasus at Tiflis. Modeste was very pleased with the young man's showing his

independence: "He who senses man in the whispering of
nature or in its fearsome uprisings," Modeste wrote in his
first letter to Kutusov, who was visiting his mother in the
country, "he who senses man in the drowsy surging of the
sea or in the evil mutterings of the deep; he who sees and
imagines in the warm sunset seen through a cloudy mist
that last little cloud in capricious flight, clothed in a rosy
garment; here is passing youth, that moment of fleeting
happiness, and then the reckless, impenetrable night, and
sorrow and dismay—such men do not have to go to the
Caucasus."

Kutusov also felt the need of a congenial companion, and
it was not long before he and Modeste became bosom
friends.

Exaggerating Kutusov's talent, Modeste insisted that
since Pushkin and Lermontov (Russia's two greatest
poets), he had never found such qualities as in his latest
discovery. "In Kutusov, almost everywhere, sincerity
springs up, almost everywhere one can sniff the freshness
of a good, warm morning—all coupled with a superb technique, inborn in him." Modeste recommended him to Stassov, hoping for Stassov's acceptance of Kutusov as a valuable addition to the *Troika*—a sculptor, a painter, a
musician, and now a poet. "I dream of a 'four-in-hand,'" he
said.

And for a while Stassov did take Kutusov under his
wing, found him a historical subject for a dramatic play,
Vassily Shuisky, and supplied him with historical material
and data from his library. To keep up with Kutusov's sudden diligence, Modeste had actually begun to compose some
scenes for *Khovanshchina* when the news of Victor Hart-

mann's death from a heart attack plunged him into utter
despair. Not since his mother's death had he felt a loss so
deeply. Hartmann was to Modeste more than a friend with
whom he could pass an entertaining evening: Modeste
firmly believed that Hartmann was one of the few men of
vision who could transform Russia's architecture. Modeste
wrote to Stassov:

The wise ones console us, the fools, that though "he" is gone,
everything that he had time to create will live, and "how many
are so fortunate as not to be forgotten?" This hash (with horse-
radish for tears) is product of human ego. To hell with such
wisdom! If "he" has not lived in vain but did create, what kind
of scoundrel would revel in the thought "that he can create no
more"? No, there cannot be any peace, nor any consolation.
This is a lot of rot. If nature is only flirting with me, if she
is a cocotte, then I should not trust her and I should watch her
carefully, for at odd times she might lure me to such a degree
where even the sky seems as mere nothing. Or should one
rather like a brave hussar, charge into the thick of life and die,
but first enjoy life to the full? Enjoy what? The flabby cold
earth, which now, not with coquetry but with true desire, ac-
cepts into her lethal embraces each "King of Nature," no matter
who he is, like an old, worn-out hag for whom anyone is good
enough since she has no choice.

This outburst of impotent wrath was caused by
Modeste's illogical feelings of guilt. During Hartmann's last
visit to St. Petersburg, Modeste had walked home with him
after an evening at the Molas'. Suddenly, Hartmann leaned
against a wall and turned pale. "I can't breathe," he whispered. "Rest a bit, my dear, and then we will go on,"
Modeste said.

"That was all that was said about something that has

hidden one so dear to us forever beneath the earth," he wrote to Stassov. "What a fool man is! And now when I recall this conversation, I feel wretched that I behaved like a coward in face of the sickness." Modeste knew from his own experience, so he said, that it was *palpitato cordis*, and yet he was afraid of frightening Hartmann and "behaved like a silly schoolboy." "I remember, I well remember the incident, and I hope I shall remember it—I may grow wiser. . . ."

Modeste not merely remembered it, he was haunted by it. With his friends away from the city, more and more often he took to drinking as his only solace. Borodin heard that Modeste was suffering from hallucinations and that he disappeared for days at a time. It was also reported that he had been seen in the suburbs of the city engaged in a brawl so violent that the police had to be called.

Alarmed by Modeste's condition, Stassov begged his friends in St. Petersburg for news of Moussorgsky. It was not reassuring: Modeste was selling most of his belongings and even his clothes, about which he had been so meticulous, he had been turned out of his apartment because he could not pay the rent and no one knew where he was living. Stassov remembered that early in the year Modeste had told him that he thought he was suffering from fits of insanity. It added further to Stassov's anxiety.

Stassov had never wholeheartedly approved of Modeste's close friendship with Kutusov. Kutusov, constantly brooding over life's being an endlessly boring existence in which death was the only solution to all problems, was not the man to save Moussorgsky from the pit into which he was sinking. Stassov thought of Franz Liszt, whom he knew

Moussorgsky admired, and he wrote to Modeste to offer a meeting with Liszt. Aware that Modeste's financial situation would prohibit any kind of journey, Stassov delicately suggested that he would pay all the expenses of the trip as a loan that Modeste could repay later, after his *Boris* had been produced, or some works published, or at any other time.

A month passed without a word from Modeste, who used to write to Stassov every day when he was in St. Petersburg. Stassov telegraphed the invitation. Moussorgsky replied with one word: "Impossible." And later Modeste wrote. He expressed over and over again his gratitude for all of Stassov's kindness, and he explained that he could not take the trip because his superior at the office was not well, and he would have felt bad, he said, if he deserted a man so swamped with work.

But there was no doubt that for a moment a bright ray of hope had passed through Moussorgsky's weary mind as he thought of the possibility of seeing Liszt:

This is what a Russian musician must answer. To refuse the most wished-for, the most living thing, to go on plodding through rubbish instead. Frightful! . . . because it is true. . . . And what might have been said during a meeting with Liszt, how many good things might have been done! You will see Liszt. I would like to ask you, my dear, to hand him a little note from me, but . . . in the first place, do I have the right to act this way, and in the second place, what would this note mean to him? However, I trust in my star; it is surely not impossible that some time or other I will meet the great men of Europe face to face. If this does not happen, I will endure it, as I endure it now. . . . Only one rich, living impression remains from your plan, as if I could see Liszt, hear him, and talk with him and with you. This is not a dream, not an irresponsible phrase. There is still enough living strength to raise in myself the mighty image of this European artist, to think of all that has been done by this artist and in a single blink of the eye to stand before him, to look at and listen to him.

But when you return, I do not ask you not to remind me that I had failed to see Liszt; on the contrary, I wish you to remind me more and more often: once in a while a disgusting feeling brings good results, and the feeling of self-aversion in this case is salutary: let me be ashamed that I wear the official uniform of a clerk!

But Stassov would not give up his plan. Through his brothers and their mutual friends he tried to change Modeste's decision, but to no avail. "It was really incredible," Repin said. "How could that well-bred Guard officer, with his beautiful and polished manners, that witty conversationalist with the ladies, that inexhaustible punster as soon as he was left alone so quickly sell his possessions, even his elegant clothes, and descend to some cheap saloons, where he personified the familiar type of 'has-been,' where this happy chubby child with the red potato-shaped nose was already unrecognizable . . . ? Was it really he—the once impeccably dressed aristocrat, heel-clicking man of society, scented, dainty, fastidious?"

After he had returned in October, Stassov would often rescue Moussorgsky from some basement establishment or disreputable place, nearly in rags, his hair disheveled, his face swollen from alcohol. Stassov found him time and time again sitting with some shady character until two in the morning or even until daybreak. With Stassov's help he would come to—gay, amiable, and witty as ever. But after a day or two he would again vanish from everybody's sight and drink heavily.

❧ Ten ❧

O NLY a production of *Boris Godunov* could rescue
Moussorgsky from total physical and mental disintegration. To ward off repeated rejections by the
Board of Directors of the Maryinsky Theatre, Yulia Platonova, a well-known soprano, after securing the support for
her plan among Moussorgsky's admirers, put pressure on
the Maryinsky Theatre administration to have the opera
produced in its entirety at her *bénéfice.** Confronted with
such a request (or was it a condition for the renewal of her
contract?) from his favorite singer, Gedeonov had no alternative but to sanction the production.

The opera was scheduled for the last half of the season of
1873–74, but the jubilant mood of Moussorgsky's friends
was dampened by Napravnik, the chief conductor at the
Maryinsky Theatre. Claiming that he was swamped with
work on the operas in the repertory, he refused to take time
for rehearsals of *Boris*. Platonova thereupon organized the

* This custom, adopted from the French, of allowing an actor,
once or twice during the theatrical season, to have a performance
of his choice in which he plays a major role—all the proceeds of the
performance going to him.

rehearsals at her home, but she needed Moussorgsky's participation.

Kutusov had rented an apartment and had brought Modeste to live with him, while Stassov did everything in his power to bring Moussorgsky "back to life" so that he could accompany the singers at the piano and be useful with his advice at the rehearsals. After intensive study the company was ready within a month for Napravnik's orchestral rehearsals.

Moussorgsky attended each rehearsal, encouraged and praised the artists and the orchestra, and to everybody's surprise and even dismay not only did not argue against Napravnik's suggestions for cuts and omissions in the score, but actually showed his gratitude to Napravnik for his advice. He was so happy to see his opera at last on its way to a performance, so anxious lest something still could thwart it, that he even consented to omitting the scenes "in Pimen's cell," "the tale of the parrot in the scene between the Tsarevich and Boris," and "the clock with chimes," as well as to making several other cuts in the score.

"These gentlemen don't care to listen, they don't require a quality of impression, but only quantity," Modeste complained to Kutusov about some of their friends who disapproved of his docility. "They say I have a weak character, but they don't understand that no composer, before his opera reaches a theatrical production, can possibly judge the impression a scene may make on the audience. Meyerbeer struck out entire pages without mercy—he knew what he was doing, and he was right!"

Although he seemed to be quite happy with the progress of the rehearsals and hopeful for the success of the opera, he was restless on the eve of its première, and went into Kutusov's room. He sat down at the piano, but after striking a few chords, shut the lid of the keyboard and walked away. "No, I can't. I know it is very silly, but what can I do? I can't get tomorrow's *examination* out of my mind—what will it be?" And he spent the night pacing up and down the room with his hands clenched behind his back, deep in thought, as Kutusov said later.

On February 6, 1874, Modeste Moussorgsky's *Boris Godunov*, the people's drama, had its first public performance.

"The opera was finally presented on the stage with stupefying success. The impression it created on the audience, the singers, and the members of the orchestra was astonishing. Its success was a complete triumph for the composer." Or so stated Moussorgsky in his autobiographical sketch intended for the well-known Riemann's musical dictionary. This not exactly modest account certainly was not justified by the general reaction at the opera's première. The novel devices in recitatives and the choruses' playing as important a role as those of the individual characters left the spectators more overwhelmed and even bewildered than pleased, for they felt that there was little of the kind of music they were used to hearing in an opera and had expected from a work so praised in advance by eminent musicians. They were almost unanimous in stating that only the exceptional acting of the cast had rescued the opera and kept their attention on the stage.

But even before Moussorgsky had a chance to read the reviews his "complete triumph" was dealt a severe blow. An incident insignificant in itself caused him grief and a great deal of anxiety. The laurel wreath to be presented to the composer was said by some to have been sent by six young ladies and by others by four, but only three names were signed to the note accompaning this token of homage decorated with ribbons on which their favorite melodies from the opera were embroidered: "On to new shores! . . . to new triumphs. . . . Glory to your *Boris!* . . ."

Russians have always been demonstrative and romantic in their expressions of admiration for an artist, and there should have been nothing extraordinary in this gesture, but when Moussorgsky, who was in the audience, heard about it, he became so embarrassed that at first he was going to leave the theatre immediately, but later he agreed to remain only after he had been assured that the presentation of the wreath would take place not on the stage but in the green room after the performance.

Apparently unaware of Moussorgsky's instructions, the young ladies blamed the theatre's administration—that is, Napravnik, who had conducted the opera—for preventing the ceremony. Stassov, who had inspired the young ladies' act, fumed with indignation for such disregard for their feelings. "I implore you, do not give the press the story of the wreath," Modeste wrote to Stassov immediately after the performance. "It might bring on consequences which you least desire. *Boris* may never be performed again. I beg you, I implore you by your love for me. . . ."

But Moussorgsky's dearest friend Stassov was betrayed by Stassov the journalist. Ignoring Modeste's plea, as well as the true facts of the incident, and signing it with the initials of the three young ladies's names, Stassov wrote an open letter to the editor of the *Peterburgskiye Vedomosti*, taking the administration and Napravnik to task. Modeste was anxiously scanning the papers for reviews of his opera when he read Stassov's letter, the first press release in connection with the performance, and he completely lost his head. He wrote to Napravnik, apologizing for the incident of the wreath and for Stassov's letter, which had distressed him. "I implore you as an artist of the highest caliber not to think of me as holding a brief for such donors and such statements," and he added that he was sending a letter to the editor of the *Petersburgskiye Vedomosti*, explaining the unfortunate incident.

And indeed he made the mistake of "clarifying" the wreath story in a lengthy statement, which the newspaper printed two days later. While Modeste tried to prove his innocence, his letters furnished ample material for what now was growing into an *affaire* out of all proportion. The critics were rehashing the whole story *da capo* in all its details, ridiculing Moussorgsky's behavior at the theatre before and after receiving the wreath, and saying that he was delighted with the opportunity that enabled him to talk about himself in an important newspaper, thus adding the laurels of a journalist to those of poet and composer.

César Cui, who should have had but failed to have more delicacy than even to mention the story, included some sarcastic comments in his lengthy review of the opera. "I want to drop a few sympathetic tears on behalf of those 'few ladies' who, in their six initials [there were three] personifying the public, have become 'victims' of the incident, but I have not the heart to do it."

And he then proceeded to devote almost a whole column to lecturing on the virtue of non-public presentations of such tokens of admiration for "a beginner's" [Moussorgsky's] work, which they had not even heard. It was unfortunate that this futile polemic should have overshadowed the critics' reactions to the opera itself. To judge from the typically verbose, confusing, and meaningless accounts of critics when faced with a new work, their analyses show that they had completely missed "the point" of the opera. And even César Cui—who, more than any other critic, had for years been led by Moussorgsky through every bar of the composition, and for whom every detail of the score had been digested—could not refrain from annihilating statements in regard to the opera. "There are two principal defects in *Boris*," he summarized his elaborate verdict. "Choppy recitative and vagueness of scattered musical ideas which make the opera a *potpourri*." Cui used such hackneyed comments as "slender musical interest in many scenes, and the preference for coarse splashes of color in the tone painting." And finally he ascribed the various defects of the opera to "immaturity, to the composer's lack of self-criticism, haphazard self-complacency, and slapdash way of composing. . . ." And as if purposely intending to hurt the most vulnerable spot in Modeste's self-esteem, he closed his last sentence with "which had the similar results for Messrs Rubinstein's and Tchaikovsky's operas."

The feud between the two groups of Russian composers —the "Mighty Five," who advocated the creation of a Russian National Music, and the other, headed by Tchaikovsky, with its Western orientation—is well known. (Eventually it ended in a draw between the two factions—Russian music being the winner.) But their antagonism was also reflected in their personal attitudes. Among the

"Mighty Five," Moussorgsky was the only one who had met Tchaikovsky, just twice, and both times in St. Petersburg, when Tchaikovsky came to the capital on a short visit. At Tchaikovsky's request Moussorgsky played *The Nursery* for him at Cui's musicale, and his polonaise from *Boris Godunov* at Vasily Bessel's, the music publisher. Tchaikovsky did not care for either composition. Later, when he shared his critical opinions of the "Mighty Five" with Nadezhda von Meck, his friend and patroness, Tchaikovsky wrote to her,

His [Moussorgsky's] nature is narrow and he has no aspirations toward self-perfection. He has been too easily led astray by the absurd theories of his set [the "Mighty Five"] and his belief in his own genius. In addition to this, his nature is not of the finest quality—he likes what is coarse and ugly.

Tchaikovsky also made clear his disapproval of the "Mighty Five's" major aim in their compositions. "I have never come in contact with anything more unattractive and false than this unsuccessful attempt at dragging 'truth' into the sphere of art, in which everything is based on falsehood, and 'truth' in the everyday sense of the word is not required at all."

Obviously Tchaikovsky had failed to comprehend their credo, and while Moussorgsky did not engage in any discussions of the subject with him, he wrote to Stassov,

It is not the sound we need, not the words, nor a palette, nor chisel—no, the Devil take you all, liars, hypocrites, and *tutti quanti!* Serve us some live thoughts, carry on a live discussion with people no matter what subject you choose. You cannot

fool us with pretty words, like a rich woman passing around a
box of chocolates among her guests.

It is a matter of taste to choose between these two composers, as it would be in giving preference to one or another
author in Russian literature. I would venture to compare
their personalities and works to two great Russian authors
of the same era: Tchaikovsky to Turgenev, and Moussorgsky to Dostoyevsky. (And I might add that the critical opinions held by these authors of each other were amazingly
similar to those of the two composers.)

Leaving aside the question of the value and durability of
their works, it is self-evident that the works of Moussorgsky and Dostoyevsky had a greater influence on the composers and authors of the twentieth century than those of
Tchaikovsky and Turgenev. Moussorgsky's eminence in
musical literature was debated during his life, after his
death, and even occasionally in our time, but in summariz-
ing his great talent and works, I can only subscribe to
Claude Debussy's reference to Moussorgsky:

. . . It is apparent from these dates [Moussorgsky was born
in 1839 and died in 1881] that to become a genius he had
little time to lose. And indeed he lost none, and he will leave
an indelible impression on the minds of those who love him
or will come to love him. No one has ever appealed to the best
in us in a deeper and more tender expression. He is unique
and will remain so, for his art is free from artifice and arid
formulas. Never was refined sensitivity interpreted by such
simple means. It is like the art of a wild creature who discovers
music in each of his emotions. Neither is there ever a question
of a definite form; or rather, this form is so manifold that it
cannot possibly be likened to the recognized or orthodox forms.

It is achieved by little consecutive touches linked by a mysterious bond and by his gift of luminous intuition. Sometimes, too, Moussorgsky produces the effect of shuddering, restless shadows, which close around us and fill the heart with anguish.

Although Stassov had warned Modeste of Cui's poisonous pen, his uncalled-for remarks struck Moussorgsky like lightning. " 'Complacency!!! Slapdash way of composing!!! Immaturity!!!' Whose . . . whose, I would like to know," Modeste exclaimed.

Had Modeste's sensitive nature not been affected by the misfortunes of his past years, had his nervous system not been keyed up to such a high pitch that he spent sleepless nights before his "examination," as he called the première, he might have taken Cui's attitude more calmly and perhaps even recognized Cui's professional jealousy, since Cui's own opera, *Ratcliff*, had been a failure.

But at that time it would have been an error to expect such a reasonable reaction from Modeste. "It took the production of *Boris* to reveal myself to others and to expose their true selves to me," Modeste concluded. Moussorgsky's pride was hurt. And the last vestige of his faith in the "Mighty Five" was shaken. But Cui was not Moussorgsky's enemy, and *Boris Godunov* was all that the "Mighty Five" could have hoped to achieve in expressing their principles. What happened was that during the past few years so much had affected them that when the call came for the final test, they were no longer friends-in-arms, champions of their former ideas.

"It is not surprising," Borodin thought, "it is the natural course of things. So long as we were eggs laid by one hen —Mili Balakirev—we were all more or less alike; but when the young chicks came out of their shells, each one of them was clothed in different feathers, and when our wings had grown, each one flew in his own direction."

Moussorgsky found consolation in the reaction of the young students. Pleased to discover in the opera some of their own revolutionary ideas, they sang excerpts from *Boris* in the corridors of the universities and even in the streets. This led the government officials to prove their authority and power in matters concerning Russian arts. After ten successful performances during that year Napravnik was coerced into compelling Moussorgsky to make ruthless and inartistic cuts in the opera. "You said that we have progressed—You were lying. We are where we have always been—prison and the police," Moussorgsky reflected, when only a skeleton was left of the already revised version of the original score. Finally, after ten more performances during the following years, *Boris* was suddenly taken out of the repertory of the Maryinsky Theatre—this time because the royal family was displeased with the opera's revolutionary—that is, "politically subversive."— tenor.

After Moussorgsky's death Rimsky-Korsakov spent five years not merely "editing" but practically rewriting the score. His aim was to make the *Boris* music more palatable for his contemporaries' understanding and taste. But out of two hundred and fifty-eight pages of Rimsky-Korsakov's version, hardly twenty conform to the original *Boris*. He cut, altered modulations and harmonies, and in addition to all the retouching and embellishing, he actually took the liberty of changing the order of the last two scenes. By shifting once again Boris' death scene to the end of the opera—instead of closing the work with the *Yurodivyi's* prophesy of "troubled times" ahead—Rimsky-Korsakov distorted the very essence and the psychology of the drama. This version was given its première at the Maryinsky Theatre in 1896, but it actually did not become popular until a few years later when Feodor Chaliapin sang the title role. Rimsky-Korsakov later justified his editing in this way:

If Moussorgsky's compositions are destined to live unfaded for fifty years after his death [1881–1931] (when all his works will become property of any and every publisher), such a musicologically accurate edition will always be possible, as the manuscripts went to the Public Library on leaving me. For the present, there was need of an edition for performances, for practical artistic purposes, for making his colossal talent known.

In 1940 Dmitri Shostakovich made one more version of *Boris*. To solve the problems presented by Moussorgsky's original and Rimsky-Korsakov's version, Shostakovich made use of Modeste's first two versions (1869 and 1872). He left the original order of the scenes, but enriched the orchestration.

Borodin was right—the "Mighty Five" had fallen apart. Under the influence of the conservatory, where he taught and also for the first time studied theoretical subjects, Rimsky-Korsakov became the composer we know, but radically different from the Rimsky-Korsakov of the Balakirev group. He had learned to appreciate the classics in musical literature, as well as to admire Bach, Palestrina, and the old Italians.

When I remember certain composers who are now behind the fence, not only sorrow overcomes me, but a sort of nausea for their desire and aspirations, dripping from their pen drop by drop, so evenly, so regularly. It pleases them, but to a real man it is a bore.

Modeste wrote to Stassov. It was his farewell to his former colleagues:

For God's sake, can't they let themselves go, as living people do? Show whether they have claws or fins, whether they are beasts of prey or just amphibians! Without any sense, without any will, they have bound themselves by tradition, these artists, and yet they imagine that they are still doing something.

All this would be of very little interest and merely unpleasant, if they, these artists, had not once taken up the banner, trying to "lift it up proudly before human society." Caught up in the middle of the road by the iron fist of Balakirev, they began to breathe with his mighty lungs, though not to the full size of his giant chest. They challenged tasks that have troubled great minds. Then Balakirev's fist loosened, and they felt that they were tired, that they needed rest. Where could they find this rest? In tradition, of course—"As our fathers have done, so will we do."

They put the glorious fighting banner in a safe place, hid it carefully, and locked it behind seven doors with seven keys. They have rested and rested. Without the banner, without an aim, without the desire to look into the future, they pore over what was done long ago and no longer want it. And so, from time to time, the critical frogs, croaking contentedly in their inherited rotten swamps, present these artists with their praise. How else can it be? The "Mighty Five" has hatched into a horde of soulless traitors. Their scourge has become a child's toy whip.

Moussorgsky was just as firm, just as fanatically devoted to his belief in the true artist's aim as before. But his voice was no longer heeded. Modeste felt keenly his former friends' indifference, and he withdrew within himself, withdrew into the introspective world that life with Kutusov had opened to him. They had set up housekeeping in Kutusov's new two-room apartment. Moussorgsky resumed his office duties, but the rest of the time they passed together. Kutusov had no particular philosophy of life. He lived within the small world of his own emotions, and he too felt the need for intimate companionship. Sentimental and warm-hearted, he was just the man to whom Moussorgsky could pour out his heart.

Modeste admired Stassov and was devoted to him, but he could not find in Stassov a sympathetic listener, for Stassov would rather change the subject to something more sensible in his opinion—for instance, a discussion of Modeste's current work. But Kutusov not only listened night after night to Moussorgsky's detailed account of his personal life, his hopes and misfortunes, but was able to reflect Modeste's disappointments and loneliness in his own pessimistic poetry. Eventually, Modeste recognized, as if in a mirror, his own state of mind in Kutusov's poems, and he set some of these poems to music.

He composed two cycles of songs—*Sunless* and, later, *Songs and Dances of Death*. The titles of the six songs of the first cycle clearly indicate Moussorgsky's loneliness: "Within Four Walls," "Thine Eyes in the Crowd Ne'er Perceived Me," "The Useless Day Is Over," "Ennui," "Elegy," and "On the River."

"Many prattle," Modeste said to Kutusov, "that the only good things in me are my placidity and sense of humor. Let us see what they will declare now, when I hand them your verses."

Contrary to Modeste's prediction of Kutusov's future as a great poet, his poetry and his name are immortal only because of Moussorgsky's music written for his texts.

Modeste was constantly working on *Khovanshchina*, but he found the time and strength, he said, to pay homage to his dead friend Victor Hartmann. In January, 1874, Stassov had organized a memorial exhibition of Hartmann's watercolors, drawings, and sketches at the St. Petersburg Architects Association. But at the time of the exhibition Modeste was so emotionally involved with the production of *Boris* that he let several months pass before he could focus his mind on a composition inspired by Hartmann's works.

It would be an error to regard Moussorgsky's composition as a photographic musical reproduction of Hartmann's works. Among the four hundred items listed in the catalogue of the exhibition there were actually only three that appear among Moussorgsky's ten short numbers in his piano-suite: "The Ballet of Chicks in Their Shells," "A Hut on Chicken Legs," and "The Great Gate of Kiev."

The first of the three was Hartmann's design for costumes in the ballet *Trilby*, based not on George du Maurier's plot (which did not appear until 1895), but on "Trilby, or the Elf of Argyle," a short story by Charles Nadier, published in 1822. (The full-length ballet, choreographed by Marius Petipa, was given its première at the Bolshoi in 1877.)

The "Hut on Chicken Legs" is traditionally the home of

Baba-Yaga of the Russian fairy tales. Moussorgsky's picture represents one of Baba-Yaga's rides on a broomstick, as he had already visualized it in his "Night on Bald Mountain."

And Moussorgsky's last picture in his piano suite has nothing photographically resembling Hartmann's design for the great Gate of Kiev, which, incidentally, originally scheduled to be erected in 1869, was never built.

Thus Moussorgsky's *Pictures* were the pure product of his fantasy—he was inspired by some sketches and drawings that he had seen not at this exhibition but at Hartmann's home. Since in his "Promenades," interspersed among the various numbers of his suite, he intended to portray himself and his impressions while walking in the gallery, he had placed, so to speak, the sketches and drawings he had seen at Hartmann's home on the walls of the gallery —perfectly legitimate poetic license.

"Gnomus," the first picture after the opening Promenade, was inspired by Hartmann's design of a small nutcracker, a children's toy made for a Christmas tree at the St. Petersburg Artists Club in 1869. It is closely related to Moussorgsky's visions of an unfortunate afflicted man such as he had shown in his song "Savishna," and the "Yurodivy" in his *Boris Godunov*.

"Il Vecchio castello" was again the product of Moussorgsky's own fantasy. Among Hartmann's sketches or drawings there were none of castles, but a few designs of fifteenth-century mansions.

"Tuileries (Dispute d'enfants après jeux)" is Moussorgsky's free development of Hartmann's pencil drawing of one corner of a garden, deserted, and without children.

"Bydlo," which in Polish means cattle, is not mentioned in the catalogue of the exhibition. Most probably Moussorgsky saw at Hartmann's home a drawing of a heavy peasant cart drawn by two big oxen.

Moussorgsky wrote to Stassov on "Wednesday, some day or other in June, '74":

Hartmann is boiling as *Boris* boiled. The sounds and ideas hung in the air, and now I am gulping and overeating. I can barely manage to scribble them on paper. I am writing four numbers— with good transitions (on *"promenade"*). I want to do it as quickly and with as few interruptions as possible. My image can be seen in these *intermezzi*.

"Promenade" (*in modo russico*), "Gnomus," "Il Vecchio castello," "Tuileries (*dispute d'enfants après jeux*)," and—right between the eyes—*"Sandamirsko bydlo"*—*"le telègue,"* [Moussorgsky's own gallicism of the Russian word *telega*, a peasant's cart]. Naturally, *le telègue* is not mentioned by name, this is just between us.

Now I should like to add Vityushka's [endearing diminutive for Victor] Jews."

Moussorgsky had composed on Jewish themes three times previously. While spending the summer of 1863 in the village of Volok, he composed "The Song of King Saul Before the Battle" on a text from one of Byron's "Hebrew Melodies." Although the principal theme was of Biblical nature, Modeste had written it with purely Slavic intonations and, in fact, had used the themes sung in the Russian Orthodox Church. And in 1866, based again on Byron's "Hebrew Melodies," he composed a chorus, "The Destruction of Sennacherib," which Balakirev had performed in 1867 at the Free Music School. In 1867 a Jewish family who lived opposite the house where Moussorgsky was staying, often gathered in the courtyard, and Modeste listened to their singing. Later he wrote the "Hebrew Song" for voice with piano accompaniment on a text by the Russian poet Lev Mey. Moussorgsky was so fascinated by the Jewish melodies that he often visited the synagogues.

But Moussorgsky was not destined to compose without interruption. He had barely completed the first half of *Pictures at an Exhibition*, when, on June 29, 1874, Nadezhda Opochinina died. How this blow, coming a year almost to the month after Hartmann's death, affected Modeste was not revealed to his friends, for he always refrained from discussing his relationship with her. In none of his letters —and he corresponded constantly—is there even the slightest hint. But there is no doubt that of all the misfortunes he had suffered this was the most disastrous. He left this "Epitaph" for voice with piano accompaniment, "dedicated to N.P.O. . . . chi . . . a":

CRUEL DEATH

Lento Cantabile

Mean, cruel death like a vulture's talons attacked your heart and killed you. Executioner, damned through the ages, has snatched even you away. Oh, if all those to whom my lament may seem insane could have only understood your soul! Oh, if they could have listened to you in conversation, or in a heated argument! Perhaps with a lofty thought I could draw for these people

Con delicatezza

Your serene image illuminated by your love of truth, your inquisitive mind observing the people calmly. You broke away in time from the glitter of society, from the "ties of habit"; you parted from it all without anger, and with clear understanding you learned a different life.

Moderato
When at my mother's death the cruel blows of fate drove me from home into a cheerless exile, when, weary and embittered by suffering, I knocked at your pure heart, hesitating and shy, like a frightened child, begging for admission, craving help—No, I cannot—I cannot go on—

A sad melody, grieving over lost love, breaks off with *a tempo primo*.

❧ *Eleven* ❧

I T would have been natural to expect Moussorgsky's complete collapse. But perhaps it had to take time before the impact of the grief could manifest itself in full force. Or was it so profound that it left him numb? There is no way of judging. His conduct only showed extraordinary self-control.

He worked on *Pictures at an Exhibition*. Two days before Opochinina's death he wrote to Stassov about the first part of his composition, and three days after her death, on July 1, 1874, he announced to him that he had completed the second half. He had added five more "pictures," and in his manuscript he wrote his own description of each episode.

A rich Jew wearing a fur hat; Sandomir and a poor Sandomir Jew. [Hartmann's two separate drawings of the rich and poor Jews were supposed to have belonged to Moussorgsky. The additional specification of Sandomir Jews originated from the fact that they were drawn by Hartmann in Sandomir, a small town in Poland where he had spent a month in 1868.]

"Limoges. *Le marché. La grande nouvelle: M. Puissangeout vient retrouver sa vache 'La Fugitive'! Mais les bonnes dames de Limoges ne sont pas tout à fait d'accord sur le sujet, parce que Mme. de Remboutsac s'est appropriée une belle denture en porcelaine, tandis que M. Panta-Pantaléon garde toujours son nez gênant—couleure pivoine.*"

In his letter to Stassov, Moussorgsky said that he believed that the second part of the composition contained the best things. "The Limoges gossips at the market is an enchanting *scherzino*, and very pianistic."

Catacombs. *Sepulcrum romanum. Con mortuis in lingua mortua* [with the dead in a dead language].

"It should have a Latin text," Moussorgsky wrote on the margins of the manuscript of his score. "The creative spirit of the departed Hartmann leads me toward skulls and invokes them—the skulls begin to glow faintly."

Was this an echo of his interest in spiritualism, to which he had first been introduced when reading Lavater's *Letters* in 1858? Moussorgsky never lost his interest in spiritualism and quite often attended seances with Stassov's brother Dmitri and Kutusov.

"Then comes Baba-Yaga—excellent and powerful," he continued in his letter to Stassov, "and finally 'The Kiev Gate' —in the manner of a hymn *à la Slavsya* [in Glinka's *A Life for the Tsar*], of course a million times weaker, but all the same a mighty and original thing. There is a particularly beautiful church motif, 'As you are baptized in Christ,' and the ringing bells that are in a completely new style."

Having completed *Pictures at an Exhibition* with these detailed comments, Moussorgsky assured Stassov that this was not his only work: "Now all of a sudden there has awakened within me such a desire for composing that apparently not a day passes without it."

He was referring to his plan for a comic opera, *The Fair at Sorochinsk*, inspired by one of the stories in Gogol's *Evenings on a Farm near Dikanka*. "*Khovanshchina* is not dozing," he reported to Stassov. "But the work on this new opera is a measure of the economy of creative strength. Two heavyweights, *Boris* and *Khovanshchina*, in succession might be crushing." Thus, the comic opera with its entirely different characters and locale—the Ukraine—was refreshing to him.

"Creative moods are as elusive and even more capricious than the most capricious coquette. One must catch them as they come, and yield completely to their capricious commands." Moussorgsky was trying to appease his friends, who were worried that in his zeal for composing he was attempting too many subjects at the same time and perhaps to the detriment of *Khovanshchina*, his major work. For after having written three of the songs in the Sunless cycle, he composed in the fall of 1874 "The Forsaken One," a song for voice with piano accompaniment.

He had been deeply moved by Vassily Vereshchagin's painting of the same name. A pacifist, Vereshchagin had portrayed the cruelty and futility of wars. "The Forsaken One," depicted a single Russian soldier left (after a victorious war) to die, lying on his back in a deserted battlefield with swarms of black crows hovering over him. The painting had caused trouble with the government, and Alexander II's order to remove the canvas from Vereshchagin's exhibition further aroused Moussorgsky's enthusiasm for the painting. In collaboration with Kutusov, Modeste wrote one of their finest dramatic songs.

Though Stassov, who until then had tried to sway Modeste from Kutusov's influence and his constant preoccupation with the theme of death, later claimed that it was he who had suggested to Moussorgsky that he compose a series of songs on the theme of Songs and Dances of Death.

As long as Modeste could remember he had always had an aversion to death: it made him shudder, not from fear but from disgust. Death had deprived him of his first love, later of his mother, and more recently of Hartmann and Opochinina. It seemed to him always to come prematurely, destroying every hope, every vestige of life. He despised it because it was unjust, using any means, and from it no man was ever safe.

He was familiar with Liszt's Danse Macabre, Schubert's Erlkönig, and Berlioz' Dies Irae. But Moussorgsky wished to depict in his songs that last struggle between man and death, between the King of Nature and his never to be conquered enemy. So far he had already succeeded in the dramatic portrayal of such a struggle in the *Boris* death scene, and now in the two first songs of the cycle, "Trepak" and "Cradle Song," he depicted death's treacherous ways of gaining his aim.

Moussorgsky continued working on the first act of *Khovanshchina*, which was almost completed, but he had given up *Fair at Sorochinsk*. "The reason for this," he claimed, "lies in the impossibility of a Great Russian posing as a Little Russian [the Ukraine is also called Malorrossiya— Little Russia] and therefore in the impossibility of mastering the Little Russian recitative—that is, all the shades and peculiarities of the musical contours in Little Russian speech. In a character opera the recitative must be approached even more carefully than in a historical opera, for in the former there is no major historical event to cover whatever inaccuracies and faults there might be." Actually, this was only a temporary discouragement, for Moussorgsky returned again and again to the score of *Fair at Sorochinsk* until the last years of his life.

Most probably the interruption of his work on *Fair at Sorochinsk* was caused by a sudden, dramatic event. There are two versions to the pitiful beginning of the last period of Moussorgsky's life.

In a letter to Stassov, who was attending a geographical congress in Paris, Moussorgsky explained his new address by simply saying that since Kutusov had forgotten to leave the key to their apartment when he left for the country, where he usually spent his summers, he was compelled to be "boarding at the expense of Pavel Naumov, a very kind friend." That Kutusov actually had forgotten to leave the key must have been true, because in a letter written ten days later to Kutusov (August 17, 1875) Moussorgsky said:

Pyotr [Kutusov's brother] was here, could not find the key (as I could not), committed the violence of breaking down the door, and lodging himself in your apartment. I, on the other hand, at five o'clock in the morning on the day of your departure, dragged my feet to Naumov's, where I found refuge, having warned him that I am afraid to be *alone*.

The other version was told by Naumov's niece:

Moussorgsky, hopelessly in arrears in his rent, came home to find his suitcase and personal belongings piled beside the outer door, which was locked. [Apparently the landlady used Kutusov's absence as the time for her action against Moussorgsky.] With his suitcase and empty pockets he wandered at night through the Petersburg streets and finally sat down to rest astride one of the stone lions decorating an imposing building on the Neva embankment. Here, meditating despondently on his predicament, the idea suddenly came to him: "What am I worrying about? Why, there on the other side lives my dear friend Naumov!" And so, in the middle of the night, the Naumov door was opened to the homeless Modeste Moussorgsky.

At that time Modeste gave no other reason for his nocturnal wandering and his sudden change of domicile, although he knew why. It was not a question of the key, which Kutusov could have sent him and which was no longer necessary once Pyotr moved into the apartment that his brother had been sharing with Modeste. Modeste was well aware that his visit at Naumov's was not just to be temporary, until Kutusov's return. But perhaps he talked himself into believing that everything would again be as it had been, once Kutusov returned to St. Petersburg. In none of their correspondence during the following four and a half months did either of them give the slightest hint of what was happening. Finally, on December 23, 1875, at night, "sunless," Modeste wrote to Kutusov:

My dear Arseny,
It is quiet in this room, cozy home, at the writing table—only the fireplace sputters. Sleep is a great wonder-worker for those who have tasted the sorrow of the earth; thus sleep reigns— powerful, tranquil, loving. In this silence, in the peace of all minds, all consciences and all desires—I, though adoring you, I alone threaten you.

My threat has no anger: it is calm as sleep without a nightmare. Neither goblin nor ghost, I stood before you. I should like to remain a simple, artless, unfortunate friend to you. You have chosen your path—go! You disdained all; an empty intimation, the joking sorrow of friendship, the faith in you and your thoughts—*in your creations* you disdained the cry of my heart— —and you do disdain it!

It is not for me to judge; I am no oracle, but at leisure from anxieties that are to you *alone*, do not forget "The narrow, dear, peaceful room" [the opening sentence of "Within Four Walls," the first song in the *Sunless* cycle].

And me do not curse, my friend.

Forever yours,
Modeste.

Six days later, on December 29, 1875, Moussorgsky wrote a letter to Stassov that began with the announcement of the completion of the second act of *Khovanshchina*, and was followed by:

Here is what happened, my dear. A young man became confused by all sorts of desires, and this is none other than Count Arseny Golenishchev-Kutusov. He trumped up a marriage, not just for fun, but in all seriousness. Here is another who goes on furlough, never to return. [Moussorgsky referred to Rimsky-Korsakov's marriage.] Good heavens! Here I am, spending my time with all sorts of bureaucratic nonsense, trying to grasp an idea (and happy when I catch one), while some people who do not have to do this, get married to take a burden upon themselves!

I cursed Arseny in plain language, and I was even rude to him. Let come what may, I cannot lie. He invited me to meet his betrothed [the sixteen-year-old Olga Gulevich]—I do not know her. I will not go; otherwise I would have to lie. I do not like what he is doing—and I will not go. And that is all there is to it. He says that he loves her—I still will not go. There is no need for it.

Such things drive me to work harder than ever. I shall be left alone—and alone I shall remain. I shall have to die alone—I cannot expect anyone to go with me. Ah, my dear, but it is annoying about Arseny.

But this was not a break in his friendship with Kutusov. Moussorgsky was incapable of nursing a grudge. Four months later he wrote a charming letter to Countess Golenishchev-Kutusova, congratulating her on her birthday and sending her the "Dances of the Persian Slaves" from *Khovanshchina* which he dedicated to her.

Although the reconciliation seemed to have been completed, Moussorgsky for a long time found excuses for not visiting them on their country estate. Perhaps he was too shy, too conscious of his appearance resulting from the life he led in the environment into which he had walked when he entered Naumov's home on that summer day at five in the morning.

Pavel Naumov, a few years older than Moussorgsky, was a former naval officer with whom Modeste had struck up a friendship over several glasses of cognac at Maly Yaroslavetz, a restaurant Moussorgsky frequented much too often. In his turbulent past Naumov had squandered first the fortune inherited from his parents and then his young wife's fortune, and when Modeste first met him, he was going through a sizable portion of the wealth of his sister-in-law with whom he now was living as husband and wife. Although he drank he was not a drunkard; most of the money was spent not on drinking bouts with friends, former officers of the Preobrazhensky Regiment, singers from the opera, and poor musicians, but on keeping mistresses among the ballet dancers.

He was a well-educated man, a great music and drama enthusiast, extremely hospitable, and he prided himself on being a *bon vivant* and nothing else. He lived, he said, to enjoy the good things in life—and these were wine and women.

Modeste arrived at Naumov's home at the time of reconciliation between the Naumovs, and since his sister-in-law's fortune was rapidly dwindling, she was treated with disdain. Always sympathizing with the "unfortunate one," Moussorgsky showed great tenderness in his relationship with the young woman and dedicated to her "The Misunderstood One," a song for voice with piano accompaniment. The manuscript is dated December 21, 1875, and carries this inscription: "To my dear little lady under the Christmas tree."

But the affectionate care with which he was treated at Naumov's, what he called their "petting and spoiling him," had a devastating effect on Moussorgsky. Naumov, "out of pure friendship," never let his guest lag behind at his parties—thus pleasantly leading Moussorgsky back to his dangerous passion.

Modeste was anxious to have the Naumovs meet Stassov and Shestakova, have them join their circle of friends, but neither of them showed the slightest desire to make the acquaintance of Moussorgsky's "new family." It saddened him, but there was nothing he could do about it. He had no other home and he had to accept their attitude—he was welcome as always at Shestakova's, and at Stassov's, but alone, without the Naumovs.

❧ *Twelve* ❧

THE first signs of Mili Balakirev's resurrection in music appeared early in January, 1877. For the past four years Mili had "avoided" music, blaming his preoccupation with music for all the misfortunes that had befallen him. He had never told anyone why he gave up his clerical job at the railroad office. He had accepted a post as musical supervisor in a girls' school, and to supplement the meager salary, he began giving piano lessons again, running from house to house, which he resented but had to tolerate. He showed no interest in anything his old friends had accomplished during his absence from their musical life. He wanted to pick up his musical activities where he had left off when he resigned from the Free Music School.

He brushed aside Borodin's Second Symphony and what was already composed of *Prince Igor*, and told him to rewrite his First Symphony by restoring all the fragments he himself had previously blue-penciled in the score. He could not care less for Cui's operas, and he still thought that Rimsky-Korsakov, his onetime favorite, could only develop other people's ideas. And as for Moussorgsky, he held to his opinion of him as a "drivelling idiot."

Stassov and, even more, Shestakova hoped that with Mili's return the old cooperation of the "Mighty Five" could be resurrected. "Surely," Stassov agreed with Shestakova, "these great, talented men were not going to drop their unique collaboration because of some trivial thing that had come between them."

As in the old days Shestakova arranged their musical evenings at her home. But the old spirit was gone. Balakirev wrote to Stassov:

I was pleasantly surprised by Modeste. No swagger or anything in the way of self-adoration; on the contrary, he was very modest, listened seriously to what was said to him and did not protest at all against the need for *knowing harmony*. He did not even jibe at the suggestion that he work at it with Korsinka [Rimsky-Korsakov].

And then, with his typical superior air and dictatorial manner he added:

For the present I have started him on a good piece of work, revising and rewriting the old score of his Witches' Sabbat, which he had left with me [seventeen years before]. There are such powerful and beautiful things in it that it would be a pity to leave it in its present disorder. I will write you after our second meeting with him.

Needless to say, the second meeting for Mili's re-examination of Moussorgsky's score never took place.

Even Stassov, who was at first spurred on by Shestakova's endeavors to salvage what was left of the old group's mutual work, was weary and gave up his plans for Mili to "shepherd the flock" again.

Far more alarming was Moussorgsky's condition deriving from his life at the Naumovs'. Although in the past two and a half years he had managed to complete the second act of *Khovanshchina* and to work occasionally on *Fair at Sorochinsk*, his entire dependence on Naumov's way of living brought him to such physical disintegration that it frightened Shestakova, who wrote to Stassov:

All this while I have been silent about him, because I did not want to distress you.

For several days last week, almost every day, he appeared at my house looking dreadful and stayed for a long time. Seeing that things were getting worse, I felt I had to do something and in order to save him and to protect myself, I wrote him a letter, asking him not to call on me when suffering from his "nervous irritation," as he calls it.

It is possible that Shestakova was kept in ignorance of the true nature of his "nervous irritation," but it is also possible that even after he had had a hemorrhage at her house and was aware of an approaching attack of epilepsy, Modeste was seeking her home in preference to Naumov's.

"I wrote him everything in a letter," Shestakova continued her report to Stassov, "but of course I put it as gently as I could, and so, last night my dear Musinka [Shestakova's endearing name for Modeste] appeared completely *comme il faut*, and gave me his word never to distress me again."

Apparently, Moussorgsky had appeared at her home drunk.

She closed her letter hoping that "for some time, at least, he would keep himself in hand," and wishing that "there was only some way of pulling him away from Naumov."

Two months later Balakirev wrote to Stassov: ". . . Moussorgsky is such a physical wreck that he can hardly become more of a corpse than he is at present."

In January, 1879, Rimsky-Korsakov conducted at a Free Music School concert the first performance of the scene in Pimen's cell that had always been omitted from the production of *Boris Godunov*. In his memoirs Rimsky-Korsakov gave a detailed account of Moussorgsky's behavior at the rehearsal. Under the influence of alcohol or simply for the sake of showing off, recalls Rimsky-Korsakov, he behaved in a quiet manner and his conversation was frequently muddled. He listened with great earnestness to the music, constantly going into raptures over the playing of the individual instruments, often in the most commonplace and insignificant passages, sometimes bowing his head pensively, sometimes throwing up his hands with a theatrical gesture. When at the end of the scene the gong was struck *pianissimo*, imitating a monastery bell, Moussorgsky made the player a deep and respectful bow, crossing his hands on his chest.

And yet Modeste not only worked simultaneously on *Khovanshchina* and *Fair at Sorochinsk*, but he was already making plans for another opera.

The contretemps in his friendship with Kutusov had long been forgotten, and since Kutusov's dramatic play *Unrest*, originally called *Czar Vassily Shuisky*, was being published, Moussorgsky now urged him to write another drama. As a subject for the play he suggested the "life campaigners"—a company of grenadiers in the Preobrazhensky Regiment who were sent by Catherine the Great against Pugachev's uprising. "Talk it over with Stassov," he advised Kutusov, "and I (if I am still alive) will compose an opera on it. Only do not think that I am pushing you toward history on my account. No . . . but it would be pleasant to work on the basis of your ideas. Let us hope so."

The idea of using the story of Yemelyan Pugachev's uprising in 1773 was not a "new idea" with Moussorgsky. Three years earlier he had discussed the subject with Stassov when he had thought of basing his opera on Pushkin's well-known *The Captain's Daughter*, dealing with the Pugachev revolt. But now he hoped to treat the uprising as another manifestation of the people's intolerance of persecutions by the government authorities. As in *Boris* and *Khovanshchina*, Moussorgsky was once more going to present the people not as a rebellious mob, but as the righteous Russian people. With *Boris Godunov* and *Khovanshchina* this new opera *Pugachevchina* would have formed a trilogy. But even if Kutusov had responded favorably to the project, it is doubtful that Moussorgsky was well enough for such a task.

Life had given Moussorgsky so much suffering, so little happiness, happiness even in its smallest manifestation. Moussorgsky was the most generous of authors—he never failed to dedicate his latest work to persons sometimes unworthy of the gift—and yet in those days, when each word of encouragement, respect, and sympathy meant so much to him, he was deprived of even a small token of Kutusov's friendship. In memory of Moussorgsky's enthusi-

asm and valuable advice on his dramatic play, Kutusov had
dedicated *Unrest* to him, but because of negligence on the
part of a clerk in the publishing firm, the dedication was
not printed. Surely this was a small matter, but it hurt
Moussorgsky deeply, weighed down as he was with so
much torment.

In his lucid moments, now more and more restricted to
short periods in which he was not drowning his loneliness
with alcohol, Moussorgsky composed three songs, which
can be regarded as "timely" and autobiographical. The
first, "Not Stricken by God's Lightning," was composed on
March 5, 1877, on Count Alexei Tolstoy's text, describing
the slow but pitiless erosion of misfortune, thus envying the
man who is killed by lightning. This was followed two
weeks later by another song, also on a Tolstoy text, "Is It
Becoming for a Brave Man to Weave or Spin?" which mir-
rored Moussorgsky's own situation of being condemned to
spend his remaining strength on a dull clerical job.

During 1878 he once more mourned his loneliness in a
song, "The Wanderer," on Alexei Pleshcheyev's text:

> Shades of lofty mountains
> o'er the waters fall,
> Seagulls white are circling far away,
> There is none left close to me
> or I would have hugged him so tight to me.

Fate was not kind to Moussorgsky. On March 2, 1878,
the famous basso Ossip Petrov, to whom Moussorgsky was
devoted, died at the age of seventy-one. Of Gypsy and
Ukrainian origin, Petrov was even in his old age a champion of Russian nationalism in opera. He was the first to

sing the leading roles in Glinka's *A Life for the Tsar* and *Russlan and Ludmilla*. Moussorgsky called him a "grand old grandpa."

It was at Petrov's home that Moussorgsky had stupefied his friends with his extraordinary musical memory. When Petrov received the score of Wagner's *Siegfried*, Moussorgsky sight-read the opera, and when he was asked to repeat the second act, he played and sang the entire Wotan scene from memory. He performed a similar feat when, coming directly from the première of Rubinstein's *Demon*, he played and sang from memory the most characteristic sections of the opera.

Petrov's death affected Moussorgsky deeply. He sat opposite Petrov's coffin sobbing like a child. Then he whispered to Nikolai Kompaneisky, an old friend from the Preobrazhensky Regiment who also happened to be in the room, "With Grandpa's death I have lost everything. I have lost the support of my whole bitter life. In his home I felt like one of the family. I have lost my irreplaceable guide. He nourished me with artistic truth and inspired my creative ability. In that coffin lies the fate of the scarcely blossoming Russian opera. From now on it will again be overgrown by foreign weeds, and for a long time they will stifle our green shoots. So be it . . ." and Moussorgsky again broke into sobs.

This loss killed his enthusiasm for *Fair at Sorochinsk*.

Moussorgsky could not find relief for his misery in the flattery that religion pays to the human heart and mix philosophical conceptions with an arbitrary symbolism that cannot withstand logic, as Balakirev had done. He could not face his dilemma alone, and he preferred the company of those who, if they did not understand the "Holy Thing," his music, were willing to listen and not argue, judge, scold, or comfort him. And where else could he find such company if not at Maly Yaroslavetz's, where he was always welcome and had good credit?

Not in the main room of the restaurant where the customers lunched or dined, but in the room in the back, separated by a heavy drapery, Moussorgsky used to join his friends at a table laden with bottles and plates of sausage, cheese, and cucumbers. While emptying glasses of cognac or vodka, or bottles of wine or beer, men regaled the company with stories of their past exploits which brought forth roars of laughter, only to be interrupted by a more serious tale of life in Siberia, hard labor, and the fate of the "unfortunates" exiled there. Sometimes the operatic basso Vladimir Vassiliyev would suddenly hold everybody's attention by raising his voice, hoarse from drinking: "Napravnik is fierce! He keeps you tight as a string! Try to miss a rehearsal, and he'll pick you to pieces."

On hearing the familiar name of Napravnik, Moussorgsky, who was holding a newspaper before his eyes, would turn his head for an instant toward the basso. "Brothers, I love Lent," Vassiliyev roared on. "Then all you do is sing 'God bless you' in church. With no Napravnik to watch you or smell your breath." And Vassiliyev would empty a tea glass of vodka in one gulp.

Moussorgsky had heard it all many times. He would turn back to his newspaper, but from the way his bleary eyes scanned the printed page, it was evident that he was not reading a single line. Resting his back against the chair, he would sway from side to side and occasionally snort loudly. If someone tried to arrange his chair more firmly on the floor so that he would not lose his balance, the rest of the company would shake their heads with disapproval: "You'll knock him over. Don't bother him. Let him alone."

And alone Moussorgsky was left when it was getting late and the company had noisily abandoned the restaurant. The waiters would clear the tables, careful not to disturb him. He was half asleep. Leaning on their brooms as they swept the floor, they whispered to each other about him: "His music has been played at the Maryinsky Theatre. Yes, sir." "When I die, you will speak of me with pride," Moussorgsky would mutter confidently, and the waiters would nod sympathetically.

Moussorgsky was grateful for any attention. Through Naumov's wide acquaintance with the students at the university, he was often asked to be accompanist at the singers' benefit performances. He was as poor as any of the needy students, and yet he contributed his services free of charge. No one, however, was sure that he would appear on the scheduled date. And the students would send a messenger to bring him to the hall in the afternoon before the evening performance.

At one of these student concerts an Italian singer, Ravelli, consented to appear on the program, but asked for an early rehearsal with the accompanist. Vassily Bertensson, who told this story, was one of the organizers of the concert, and he was lucky to find Moussorgsky at home during the afternoon of the performance. Modeste was drunk, and he quietly but firmly refused to go to see the

Italian singer: "*Non, monsieur, non; maintenant c'est impossible. Ce soir je serai exacte.*"

When drunk, Moussorgsky often insisted on speaking French with those whom he considered well-educated. Promptly at seven in the evening he came to the hall where the concert was to take place. While waiting for Ravelli, he remained in the green room sampling the drinks on the table. But when Ravelli, claiming that his voice was a little strained and that he would therefore like to sing his program half or even a whole tone lower, Moussorgsky simply said, "*Pourquoi pas?*" And, at their quick rehearsal he so charmed Ravelli with his refined performance and his ability to transpose to any key that Ravelli embraced him, exclaiming, "*Ah, che artista, che artista!*"

This and similar feats during his frequent appearances at the student evenings made Moussorgsky so popular that a benefit performance without his participation would have been unthinkable. "If worse comes to worse," Moussorgsky wrote to Stassov, "I can always earn a living by banging the keyboard." It was a ray of hope, not for "living" but for existing. What he wanted was to be able to live as a composer, not as a keyboard "*tappeur.*" He wanted to give himself over entirely to his art. Had he not proved that his one aim was to serve his art? Was this not reason enough to be granted a living?

❧ *Thirteen* ❧

MOUSSORGSKY complained about intrigues against
him in his office, when actually it was his irregu-
larities and his shocking appearance that cost him
his job. "What of it?" he sneered in utter contempt. *Khovanshchina* was progressing very well, and he kept his head
high.

Stassov begged Mili Balakirev to save Moussorgsky. Reluctantly, Mili turned to his friend Tert Fillipov, the government comptroller, for help. Despite the unflattering
"very glad," scribbled on Moussorgsky's discharge papers
by his former chief, Fillipov managed to obtain for Modeste
a small clerical post in one of his offices. It was due only to
Fillipov's indulgence—"I am a servant of artists," he used
to explain—that Moussorgsky's "work" was tolerated.
Eventually, his functions were restricted to visits to the
office to collect his salary. Moussorgsky, always most con-
scientious where "duty" was concerned, now did not care.

Ten years older than Moussorgsky and the foremost contralto at the Maryinsky Theatre, Daria Leonova had been

an opera and concert singer for more than twenty-five years. Having completed a successful concert tour abroad, she planned another one through the provincial towns as far south as Sebastopol, as far west as Odessa, and as far east as Voronezh and Tambov, and she invited Moussorgsky to join her. His major role was to be her accompanist, but as was customary, he also would have to appear as soloist in a few numbers on each program.

When Shestakova, Stassov, Rimsky-Korsakov, and a few friends who still cared about Moussorgsky heard about it, they were indignant: it would be degrading for Moussorgsky, the composer, to be Leonova's accompanist. Balakirev, always ready to give Moussorgsky up as a living corpse, alarmed Shestakova when he begged her to prevent this tour. Not only because of the shameful role Moussorgsky was to assume and Leonova's obvious desire to exploit him, but, above all, he explained, because of the danger of his illness: "Suppose blood pours out of him," Mili wrote Shestakova, "as once happened at your home."

But Moussorgsky was jubilant. He brushed aside the "silly" notion that as a composer he should not appear in public as an accompanist. "Anton Rubinstein does it all the time," he said. Furthermore, he was delighted because he was sure to earn no less than a thousand rubles on this tour. It would make him independent, at least for a while.

The tour lasted three months, from July 29 to October 21, 1879. Leonova at fifty was no longer the singer she had been ten years earlier, but Moussorgsky overlooked her poor taste and her craving for cheap effects. While her programs consisted of operatic arias and songs by Gounod, Schubert, Rimsky-Korsakov, and of course a large number of Moussorgsky's songs, Moussorgsky's solo numbers showed how taxing his contribution to the concerts was. Partly for the edification of the provincial audiences but also for more glamorous presentation of the compositions he performed, the titles given in the programs were high-sounding and bombastic: "Coronation of Czar Boris with Great Pealing of Bells During the People's Acclamation, a scene from the opera *Boris Godunov*"; and in the following group, "Evening Promenade of the Guests in the Garden of the Sandomir Voyevoda Mnizech (polonaise), a scene from the opera *Boris Godunov*," "Hopak of the Merry Peasant Lads, from the new opera *Fair at Sorochinsk*," and "Triumphal March of the Preobrazhensky Company of Czar Peter the Great's bodyguard, from the opera *Khovanshchina*."

It goes without saying that these compositions were always improvised and were never played the same way twice. One new piece was added to this list after their tour took them to the shores of the Black Sea. When at the end of one of their performances the audience rushed to the platform calling for encores, Leonova persuaded Moussorgsky to play his "Storm on the Black Sea." The audience was puzzled by the lack of what they called "music," but the more perceptive among the musicians discovered an "amazing perfection of onomatopoeia." When Moussorgsky reached the highest notes on the keyboard, the pealing passages completed the illusion of waves breaking against a cliff. (No sketches, if there were any, of this composition have survived.)

Thus, only one composition written during this tour was ever added to the list of Moussorgsky's works. "The Song of the Flea," based on the text of Mephistopheles' song in

Goethe's *Faust*, created a sensation when Leonova gave its first performance. To this day it remains a favorite in singers' concert repertories.

Moussorgsky wrote enthusiastic reports to his friends, but the tour was a financial disappointment. Far from earning a thousand rubles, Moussorgsky returned to St. Petersburg almost as poor as when he had left. Except for some short trips in the vicinity of St. Petersburg and Moscow, this was his first journey through Russia. He reveled in the life of a concertizing artist and in his impressions of new places and people. This was, no doubt, refreshing, but he returned to St. Petersburg completely exhausted.

Before he started on this tour he sincerely believed that if worse came to worse, he could earn his living as a pianist. His experiences during the tour brought an extra disappointment. Since Moussorgsky had not played nor practiced the piano as befits a performer, his playing evoked its former grandeur and brilliance only occasionally. Above all, he had no concert repertory.

He had no home to return to; he had given up his government post and moved from the Naumovs' to a single room in a boarding house. According to the Russian poet Apollon Maikov, who called on him once at two in the afternoon, he found Moussorgsky dressed in a frock coat and asleep in an armchair next to a dirty table covered with empty bottles and remnants of food. There was nothing else in the room.

Prompted by Stassov, his friends came to Moussorgsky's assistance by offering him a monthly income of a hundred and eighty rubles on the condition that he would complete *Fair at Sorochinsk* and *Khovanshchina* within a year. But it was too late. Since Ossip Petrov's death, Moussorgsky had lost interest in the opera, and instead, he was pulling *Khovanshchina* to pieces, throwing out fragments and even whole scenes. He busied himself with some piano transcriptions from *Boris* so that he could get money from a publisher.

During the summer of 1880 Leonova took him to her summer home near Oranienbaum. Once a week she gave a musicale with supper but thoughtlessly left the arrangements for the latter in Moussorgsky's care, and from a room in the rear one could hear the clatter of plates and the uncorking of bottles. Each time Moussorgsky came out of the room he appeared a little more drunk. Balakirev's prediction that Leonova would not be able to keep Moussorgsky from drinking was coming true. But nobody was to blame: Moussorgsky was too tightly held in the grip of his passion to claim mastery over his own life.

Nevertheless, it was at Leonova's summer home near Oranienbaum that Moussorgsky "completed" *Khovanshchina*, and there that he and Leonova made plans for a private music school in St. Petersburg. In Rimsky-Korsakov's opinion Leonova was a talented artist who had a good contralto voice, but who had actually had no schooling and was not capable of teaching the technique of singing. Her lessons consisted mainly of teaching songs and excerpts from operas. She needed an accompanist and musician who could supervise the correct practicing of songs and arias, and Moussorgsky accepted this post of *maestro*. He even taught the elementary theory of music and wrote some exercises for students which, according to Rimsky-Korsakov, were full of mistakes.

But although the school had only a few students. Nevertheless, Moussorgsky never lost hope for its success, the misery of his existence led him to the Maly Yaroslavetz more and more often.

During the last days of January, 1881, Russia mourned the death of its great author—Dostoyevsky had died on January 28. A week later Moussorgsky attended an evening at a literary club commemorating the writer. When Dostoyevsky's portrait swathed in black crepe was placed on the stage, Moussorgsky went to the piano and improvised a knell resembling that of the *Boris* death scene. The audience rose to listen to Moussorgsky's farewell to another man who had pleaded for the *Insulted and the Injured*. Nobody in the audience suspected that this was also a farewell from Russia's greatest composer to all the living. It was to be his last public appearance.

Less than a week later, on November 11, Moussorgsky rushed to Leonova in an extremely agitated state. He told her of his desperate situation: he had no more money and he had no way of earning any. Was he left no alternative other than begging in the streets? Or was he to die of starvation in the gutter?

All Leonova could do to calm him was to promise to share with him what little she had herself. That afternoon she kept him at her apartment, and in the evening, to distract him, she persuaded him to go with her to hear one of their pupils sing at her parents' home for a group of their friends. The girl sang very well, but Leonova noticed that Moussorgsky, who had offered to accompany her, played the piano in an unusually nervous way. His mind obviously was on something else. After the singing the young people danced and the other guests played cards. Moussorgsky, who had remained with the students, suddenly fell unconscious to the floor in a fit.

Fortunately, there was a doctor among the guests who helped him. After he had recovered he left the party with Leonova, and on the way to her house he begged her to let him stay at her apartment, because of "the condition of his nerves," he said, and his fear of being left alone.

Leonova arranged her small study so that he could spend the night, and instructed her servant to watch over him and to call her in case anything should happen again. Next morning the servant reported that Moussorgsky had slept the whole night in an easy chair. He breakfasted in the dining room with Leonova, however, and seemed in quite good spirits. He assured her that he felt well, but as he got up from the table he fell forward to the floor.

It was fortunate, Leonova said later, that he was at her house, for alone in his room he would have choked to death. She and the servant turned him over, gave him immediate help, and sent for a doctor. That afternoon Moussorgsky had two more fits in succession.

In the evening Leonova managed to summon Stassov and Fillipov, and they tried to persuade Moussorgsky to be taken to a hospital, where he would have the necessary care. For a while he insisted that he would rather remain at Leonova's, but when he was promised a private room, he reluctantly consented to follow their advice.

It was only then that Moussorgsky's friends openly acknowledged epilepsy as his true illness. And yet two years previously, in December, 1878, Moussorgsky had written to Kutusov that ever since the spring of that year, he had been suffering from a strange illness that had reached such a state that his doctor, Kallik, who knew him well and had been treating him, warned him that he might die within two hours.

After long consultations in which Rimsky-Korsakov, Borodin, and Cui joined, Malvina Cui asked Dr. Lev Bertensson, a friend and admirer of Moussorgsky, to put him into the Nikolaevsky Military Hospital under Bertensson's care. Since Moussorgsky was no longer considered a retired officer of the Preobrazhensky Regiment, but merely a civilian, and Bertensson was only a junior staff physician with no executive powers in the hospital, which served army personnel exclusively, Moussorgsky had to be entered in the hospital as "Dr. Bertensson's hired orderly."

To keep their promise of a private room, Bertensson succeeded in obtaining a room in the back of the hospital which at least could give Moussorgsky the illusion of privacy. In a large sunny high-ceilinged ward several empty beds were partitioned off by gray screens. In addition to Moussorgsky's bed, covered by a gray army blanket, there were two chairs, a lectern, and two small tables holding daily newspapers and a few books, among them Berlioz' treatise on orchestration, brought in at Moussorgsky's request.

Under constant medical care—he was provided with two Red Cross nurses, two male nurses, and an intern—and the warm attention of his visiting friends, who supplemented the officers' rations with delicacies, Moussorgsky not only seemed to recover but also professed to enjoy his new abode. He often told his friends that he felt as if he were in his own home, surrounded by his own family and the fondest of attentions. Since his mother's death, Moussorgsky had always craved a home of his own but had never had one.

During the following three weeks his health progressed so well that when Kutusov visited him, Moussorgsky spoke of his future plans. "I would like to do something entirely new, a subject I have never touched. I would like to have a change from history. Let us work on something important —you write a fantastic drama and I will clothe it in sounds so that not a word will be changed, just as in Dargomizhsky's *The Stone Guest*. Only, not a word about this to anybody. Let it be a secret for a while."

And when Repin came to see him and suggested painting his portrait, Moussorgsky's spirits rose even higher. For four days he posed in an armchair for the painter. The two friends carried on lively discussions on the future of the arts and the future of Russia, since Czar Alexander II had just been assassinated.

Without an easel, working on a small table, Repin completed his masterpiece just in time, for after the first week in March, Moussorgsky's health turned again for the worse. And yet in his lucid moments he still believed in his recovery and was already savoring the celebration of his approaching birthday, which he claimed was on March 16 rather than March 9. Philarète, who as if dead himself had never shown the slightest interest in his brother, now came to visit him and left him some money. It was a kind gesture, but a dangerous one. Dr. Kallik had warned that alcohol might prove fatal for Moussorgsky. The hospital attendants were strictly forbidden to procure it for him, but one of them, excusing himself by saying that "a heart is not made of stone," and for a generous gift of twenty-five rubles from Moussorgsky, brought him a bottle of cognac.

On March 14 Moussorgsky's arms and legs were paralyzed, and paralysis threatened his lungs. But with the help of medical treatment he recovered sufficiently to talk to his visitors of his plans to again go to the Crimea, to travel to Constantinople, and to entertain them with amusing stories. He demanded to be helped into the armchair: *"Il m'arrive de recevoir des dames,"* he explained. *"Il faut donc que je sois très correct, sinon qu'iraient-elles penser de moi!"*

That night he fell asleep peacefully, but at five in the morning (March 16) the night nurse heard his last words: "Everything is finished. Ah, how miserable I am!" His agony lasted less than a quarter of an hour.

Philarète showed no interest in the fate of his brother's works. Those of Moussorgsky's manuscripts that were found were turned over to Rimsky-Korsakov, but some pages of his late compositions had perished among the rubbish burned by a servant when she cleaned Leonova's summer home near Oranienbaum.

Rimsky-Korsakov "edited," rewrote, and orchestrated *Khovanschchina*. In 1915, when he was over eighty, Cui completed Moussorgsky's *The Fair at Sorochinsk*, which was given its première in October, 1917. But Russia was in the grip of the Revolution, and the première passed almost unnoticed.

Immediately after Moussorgsky's death, Stassov started a subscription for a monument to be erected over Moussorgsky's grave in the Alexander Nevsky Monastery. Repin donated the fee paid by Pavel Tretyakov for the portrait of

Moussorgsky, Rimsky-Korsakov turned over the receipts from the première of *Khovanshchina*, the sixteen-year-old Glazunov gave the prize money awarded him for his First Symphony, and the sculptor, Ginsburg, declined a fee for his work.

At the unveiling ceremony in 1885 the four corners of the veil were lifted by Balakirev, Borodin, Cui, and Rimsky-Korsakov—the four remaining members of the "Mighty Five." Under the bas-relief of Moussorgsky, at Stassov's request, an inscription from Pimen's monologue in *Boris Godunov* was engraved:

SO THAT THE DESCENDANTS OF THE ORTHODOX
MAY KNOW THE PAST FATE OF THEIR OWN LAND.

List of Moussorgsky's Works

CHORAL WORKS

Incidental music for *Oedipus* (1859)
The Destruction of Sennacherib, for chorus and orchestra (1867)
Joshua, for chorus and orchestra (1874)
Four Russian Folk Songs, for *a cappella* male choir (1880)

OPERAS

The Marriage (1868)
Borus Godunov (1868–69; revised 1871–72)
Khovanshchina (begun 1873; left almost completed; orchestrated and completed by Rimsky-Korsakov)
The Fair at Sorochinsk (begun 1874, left unfinished; completed version by César Cui, Alexander Tcherepnin, and Visarion Shebalin)

ORCHESTRAL WORKS

A Night on Bald Mountain (1867)
Turkish March (The Capture of Kars) (1879–80)

PIANO WORKS

Porte-Enseigne Polka (1852)
Souvenir d'enfance (1857)

Scherzo in C-sharp minor (1858)
Impromptu Passioné (1859)
Sonata in C major (for four hands) (1860)
Intermezzo in modo classico (1867)
Memories of Childhood: "My Nurse and I," "First Punishment,"
  "Reverie," "La Capricieuse" (1865)
Pictures at an Exhibition (1874)
On the Southern Shore of the Crimea (1880)
Meditation (1880)
Une larme (1880)
The Seamstress (scherzino) (1880)

SONGS

"Tell me, dear little star, where art thou?" (composed June 4,
  1857, to a text by Moussorgsky)
"The Joyous Hour" (drinking song, composed April 28, 1859,
  to a text by Alexei Koltzov)
"O maid, tell me why . . ." (composed July 31, 1858, to a
  text by Koltzov)
"Meines Herzens sehnsucht (composed September 6, 1858, to
  a text of Heinrich Heine)
"The leaves were sadly rustling (composed in 1858 to a text
  by Alexei Plescheyev)
"I owe many palaces" (composed in 1860 to a text by Koltzov)
"What are the worlds of love to you?" (composed in 1860 to
  a text by A. Amossov)
"The Song of King Saul Before the Battle" (composed in 1863
  to a text from Byron's "Hebrew Melodies")
"Song of an Old Man" composed August 13, 1863, to a text
  from Goethe's *Wilhelm Meister*)
"If only I could have met thee once again!" (composed August
  15, 1863, to a text by Vasili Kurochkin)
"The winds are blowing, wild winds" (composed March 28,
  1864, to a text by Koltzov)
"Night" (composed April 10, 1864, to a text by Pushkin)

"Calistratus" (composed May 22, 1864, to a text by Nikolai Nekrassov)

"Song of the Balearic Islander" (composed August 1864 to a text by Moussorgsky)

"A Prayer" (composed February 2, 1865, to a text by Lermontov)

"The Outcast" (composed June 22, 1865, to a text by Ivan Goltz-Miller)

"Sleep, sleep, peasant's son" (cradle-song, composed September 5, 1865, to a text from Alexander Ostrovsky's play *Voyevoda*)

"A Baby" (composed January 7, 1866, to a text by Pleshcheyev)

"Desire" (composed April 15/16, 1866, to a text by Heine)

"Hopak" (composed August 31, 1866, to a text by Taras Shevchenko)

"There is much that grows from my tears" (composed September 1, 1866, to a text by Heine)

"Savishna" (composed September 2, 1866, to a text by Moussorgsky)

"Ah, you drunken woodcock" (composed September 22, 1866, to a text by Moussorgsky)

"The Seminarist" (composed September 27, 1867, to a text by Moussorgsky)

"Hebrew Song" (composed June 12, 1867, to a text from the Song of Solomon, translated by Lev Mey)

"The Magpie" (composed August 26, 1867, to a text by Pushkin)

"Gathering Mushrooms" (composed August 1867 to a text by Mey)

"The Feast" (composed in late September 1867 to a text by Koltzov)

"A Naughty Boy" (composed December 19, 1867, to a text by Moussorgsky)

"The Billygoat" (composed December 23, 1867, to a text by Moussorgsky)

"By the River Don a garden blooms" (composed December 23, 1867, to a text by Koltzov)

"The Classicist" (composed December 30, 1867, to a text by Moussorgsky)

"The Little Orphan Girl" (composed January 13, 1868, to a text by Moussorgsky)

"A Children's Song" (composed April 6, 1868, to a text by Mey)

"My Nurse and I" (*The Nursery*, #1; composed April 26, 1868, to a text by Moussorgsky)

"Yeremushka's Cradle-Song" (composed March 16, 1868, to a text by Nekrassov)

"The Puppet Show" (composed June 15, 1870, to a text by Moussorgsky)

"In the Corner" (*The Nursery*, #2; composed September 30, 1870, to a text by Moussorgsky)

"The Beetle" (*The Nursery*, #3; composed October 18, 1870, to a text by Moussorgsky)

"With a Doll" (*The Nursery*, #4; composed December 18, 1870, to a text by Moussorgsky)

"Evening Prayer" (*The Nursery*, #5; composed December 18, 1870, to a text by Moussorgsky)

"Evening Song" (composed March 15, 1871, to a text by Pleshcheyev)

" 'Sailor' the Cat" (*The Nursery*, #6; composed August 15, 1872, to a text by Moussorgsky)

"The Hobbyhorse" (*The Nursery*, #7; composed September 14, 1872, to a text by Moussorgsky)

"The Forsaken One" (composed in the autumn of 1874 to a text by Arseny Golenishchev-Kutusov)

"Within four walls" (*Sunless*, #1; composed May 7, 1874, to a text by Golenishchev-Kutusov)

"Thine eyes in the crowd ne'er perceived me" (*Sunless*, #2; composed May 19, 1874, to a text by Golenishchev-Kutusov)

"The useless day is over" (*Sunless*, #3; composed May 19/20, 1874, to a text by Golenishchev-Kutusov)

"Ennui" (*Sunless*, #4; composed June 2, 1874, to a text by Golenishchev-Kutusov)

"Elegy" (*Sunless*, #5; composed August 19, 1874, to a text by Golenishchev-Kutusov)

"On the River" (*Sunless*, #6; composed August 25, 1874, to a text of Golenishchev-Kutusov)

"Trepak" (*Songs and Dances of Death*, #1; composed February 17, 1875, to a text of Golenishchev-Kutusov)

"Cradle-Song" (*Songs and Dances of Death*, #2; composed April 14, 1875, to a text by Golenishchev-Kutusov)

"Serenade" (*Songs and Dances of Death*, #3; composed May 11, 1875, to a text by Golenishchev-Kutusov)

"Cruel Death" (Epitaph; composed June 29, 1875, to a text by Moussorgsky)

"The Misunderstood One" (composed December 21, 1875, to a text by Moussorgsky)

"Field Marshal" (*Songs and Dances of Death*, #4; composed June 5, 1877, to a text by Golenishchev-Kutusov)

"Not stricken by God's lightning" (composed March 5, 1877, to a text by Golenishchev-Kutusov)

"The soul calmly floated through Heaven" (composed March 9, 1877, to a text by Alexei Tolstoy)

"Is it becoming for a brave man to weave or spin?" (composed March 29, 1877, to a text by Tolstoy)

"Grief Disperses" (composed March 21, 1877, to a text by Tolstoy)

"A Vision" (composed April 7, 1877, to a text by Golenishchev-Kutusov)

"Haughtiness" (composed May 15/16, 1877, to a text by Tolstoy)

"The Wanderer" (composed in 1878 to a text by Fr. Ruckert, translated by Pleshcheyev)

"The Song of the Flea" (composed August-September 1879 to a text from Goethe's *Faust*)

"On the River Dniepr" (composed December 23, 1879, to a text by Shevchenko)

❧ *Bibliography* ❧

"Avtobiographicheskaya zapiska M. P. Moussorgskavo," *Muzykalnyi Sovremenik*, Petrograd, 1917, #5–6.

BASKIN, V. "M. P. Moussorgsky," *Biographicheskii ocherk, Russkaya Mysl*, Year 5, Moscow, 1885, Vols. 9, 10.

FINDEIZEN, N. F. "Biographia M. A. Balakireva," *Russkaya muzykalnaya gazeta*, St. Petersburg, 1895.

———. "Moussorgsky: Evo detstvo, yunost i pervyi period muzykalnavo tvorchestva," *Ezhegodnik Imperatorskikh Teatrov*, St. Petersburg, 1911, Vols. 1, 2.

———. "Iz neizdannykh pisem N. A. Rimsky-Korsakova," *Ezhegodnik Imperatorskikh Teatrov*, St. Petersburg, 1913, Vol. 5.

FRANKENSTEIN, ALFRED. "Victor Hartmann and Modeste Moussorgsky," *The Musical Quarterly*, Vol. XX (1939).

GLEBOV, V. P. "M. A. Balakirev," *Istoricheskii Vestnik*, Petrograd, 1916, #3, 12.

HOFFMAN, MICHEL R. *La Vie de Moussorgski*, Paris, 1964.

KARATYGIN, V. "M. A. Balakirev," *Apollon*, St. Petersburg, 1910, #10.

———. "Rodoslovnaya M. P. Moussorgskavo po muzhskoi i zhenskoi linii," *Muzykalnyi Sovremenik*, Petrograd, 1947, #56.

———. "Nazionalnyi muzykalnyi geni," *Vseobschchi Ezhemesyachnik*, Petrograd, #5–6.

KOMAROVA, V. "Iz detskikh vospominani o velikikh lyudyakh, Moussorgsky," *Muzykalnyi Sovremenik*, Petrograd, 1917, #5–6.

LEYDA, JAY and SERGEI BERTENSSON, editors and translators, *The Moussorgsky Reader: A Life of M. P. Moussorgsky in Letters and Documents*, New York, W. W. Norton, 1947.

"Neizdanye pisma Moussorgskavo i Borodina," *Russkaya muzykalnaya gazeta*, St. Petersburg, 1897, Vol. 4.

"Neizdanye pisma Moussorgskavo k L. I. Shestakovoi i P. S. Stassovoi," *Muzykalnyi Sovremenik*, Petrograd, 1917, #5, 6.

"Perepiska M. A. Balakireva s V. V. Stassovym," Vol. 1, 1858–69, Moscow, Ogis-Muzgis, 1935.

"Pisma Moussorgskavo k A. A. Kolenischchevu-Kutusovu," Moscow, Gos. Muz. Isd., 1939.

LIAPUNOV, S. "M. A. Balakirev," *Ezhegodnik Imperatorskikh Teatrov*, St. Petersburg, 1910, Vols. 7, 8.

LUKASH, I. "Bednaya Lyubov Moussorgskavo," *Knigoizd Vozrozhdenie*, Paris, 1940.

RIMSKY-KORSAKOV, N. *My Musical Life*, New York, Alfred A. Knopf, 1942.

SABANEYEV, L. "O Moussorkskom," *Sovremenye zapiski*, Paris, 1939, Vol. 68.

SEROFF, V. I. *The Mighty Five*, New York, Allen, Towne & Heath, 1948.

STASSOV, V. V. "A. P. Borodin," *Istoricheskii Vestnik*, St. Petersburg, 1887, Vol. 28.

———. "M. P. Moussorgsky," *Vestnik Evropy*, St. Petersburg, 1881, Vol. 3.

———. "Pamyati Moussorgskavo," *Vestnik Evropy*, St. Petersburg, 1886, Vol. 23.

———. "N. A. Rimsky-Korsakov," *Severnyi Vestnik*, St. Petersburg, 1890, Vol. 12.

———. "Sobranie sochinenii: 25 let Russkovo Isskusstva," *Isskusstvo v XIX Veke.*

TIMOFEYEV, G. "Balakirev v Prage," *Sovremenyi Mir*, St. Petersburg, 1917, Vol. 6.

————. "Borodin: Zhisn, tvorchestvo, neizdante pisma," *Sovremenik*, St. Petersburg, 1912, #8 and #9.

PLATONOVA, YULIA. "Novye materialy dlya biographii Moussorgskavo," *Russkaya muzykalnaya gazeta*, St. Petersburg, 1895.

❧ *Index* ❧

Alexander II, Czar, 25, 48–50, 115, 174
Amossov, A., 39
Antakolski, Mark, 114, 116–117, 119

Bach, Johann Sebastian, 139
Bacon, Francis, 114
Balakirev, Mili, 17–18, 21–26, 28, 30–33, 39, 41, 43–45, 48–50, 53–56, 58–60, 63, 64, 67–72, 76, 78, 81–83, 85–88, 91, 94–96, 98, 105, 108–114, 137, 140, 144, 156–157, 159, 166, 167, 176
Bamberg Rafail, 27
Belinsky, Visarion, 42
Beneke, Friedrich Eduard, 114
Beethoven, Ludwig van, 22, 70, 94
Berlioz, Hector, 150
Bertensson, Dr. Lev, 173
Bertensson, Vassily, 164–165
Borodin, Alexander, 58, 59, 72, 81, 82, 87, 94, 97, 103, 105–108, 111, 112, 137, 156, 173, 176
Borodina, Ekaterina, 106
Byron, Lord, 31, 144

Catherine the Great, Czarina, 160
Chaliapin, Feodor, 139
Chernyshevsky, Nikolai, 26, 49–50, 119

Chopin, Frédéric, 18
Cui, Alexander, 17
Cui, Antoine, 16
Cui, César, 16, 17, 23, 26, 27, 29, 38, 50, 58, 59, 62, 63, 67, 69, 72, 79, 80, 81, 94, 98, 101, 103–105, 107, 133–135, 137, 156, 173, 175, 176
Cui Malvina Bamberg, 27, 29, 38, 173
Cui, Napoleon, 17

Dargomizhsky, Alexander, 12–15, 21, 27, 29, 37, 41, 63, 72, 73–76, 78–81, 86, 87, 94, 174
Debussy, Claude, 136
Descartes, René, 114
Diderot, Denis, 26
Dobrolyubov, Nikolai, 119
Dostoyevsky, Feodor, 35, 62, 136, 171
Dubuque, Alexander, 18, 22

Eizrikh, Karl, 21
Elena Pavlovna, Grand Duchess, 46, 47, 56, 96–98, 109

Field, John, 8, 18
Fillipov, Tert, 166, 172
Flaubert, Gustave, 61

Gedeonoshvili, Prince Luka, 58

(187)

: MODESTE MOUSSORGSKY :

Gedeonov, Stepan, 97, 99, 129
Ginsburg, 176
Glazunov, Alexander, 176
Glinka, Mikhail, 12–15, 21–22, 24, 33, 40, 68, 72, 74, 98, 114, 148, 162
Gluck, Christoph, 33
Godunov, Boris, 4n.
Goethe, Johann Wolfgang von, 169
Gogol, Nikolai, 26, 38, 62, 79, 80, 87, 89, 113, 149
Gorky, Maxim, 24
Gounod, Charles-François, 167

Handel, George Frederick, 21
Hartmann, Victor, 114–116, 124–126, 142–145, 147, 148, 150
Haydn, Joseph, 23
Heine, Heinrich, 62, 93
Henselt, Adolph, 8
Herke, Anton, 7–10, 73
Herzen, Alexander, 26, 41, 42, 52, 93
Hugo, Victor, 12, 62

Ivan III, Czar, 4n.

Kallik, Dr., 173–174
Kalbrenner, Friedrich, 8
Kant, Immanuel, 114
Khotinsky, Matvei, 83, 84
Khovansky, Prince Ivan, 121
Kompaneisky, Nikolai, 162
Korf, Baron Modeste A., 25
Kostomarov, Nikolai I., 4n.
Krylov, Victor, 38
Kutusov, Count Arseny Golenishchev, 123–124, 126, 130, 131, 141, 142, 150–154, 159, 160, 172, 174
Kutusov, Count Pyotr Golenishchev, 151–152
Kutusova, Countess Olga Golenishchev, 153–154

Lavater, Johann Kaspar, 32
Leibniz, Gottfried Wilhelm, 114
Leonova, Daria, 166–168, 170–172

Lermontov, Mikhail, 63, 124
Lessing, Gotthold Ephraim, 24, 26
Leschetizky, Theodor, 47
Liszt, Franz, 22, 126, 127, 150
Locke, John, 114
Lukash, Ivan, 34n.

Maikov, Apollon, 62, 169
Meck, Nadezhda von, 135
Mendelssohn-Bartholdy, Felix, 59, 71
Mengden, Baron, 43
Mey, Lev A., 78, 145
Mollas, Nicholas, 103, 125
Moniuszko, Stanislas, 17, 69
Moscheles, Ignaz, 8
Mozart, Leopold, 95
Mozart, Wolfgang Amadeus, 21, 23, 33, 79, 94, 95
Moussorgsky, Alexei, 3
Moussorgsky, Philarète (Evgeni), 4, 8, 32–34, 44, 50, 51, 53, 57, 65, 66, 79, 174, 175
Moussorgsky, Pyotr, 3
Moussorgsky, Yulia Chirikova, 3–7, 23, 50, 53, 63

Napoleon, 26, 40
Napravnik, Eduard, 99, 109, 129, 130, 132–133, 138, 163
Naumov, Pavel, 151–152, 154, 155, 158–159, 164, 169
Nekrassov, Nikolai, 26, 62
Nicholas I, Czar, 26, 46, 48, 49
Nikolsky, Vladimir, 79, 80, 88, 89, 99, 122

Opochinin, Alexander, 41, 57, 72, 73, 83, 91, 102, 123
Opochinina, Nadezhda, 41, 43, 62, 72, 83, 91–93, 102, 123, 145, 147, 150
Ostrovsky, Alexander, 64

Palestrina, Giovanni Pierluigi da, 139
Petrov, Ossip, 161, 162, 170
Peter the Great, Czar, 121
Petipa, Marius, 142
Platonova, Yulia, 129

(188)

Pleshcheyev, Alexei, 161
Pugachev, Yemelyan, 160
Purgold, Alexandra, 73–75, 81, 92–94, 97, 104
Purgold, Nadezhda, 73–75, 81, 92, 94, 97, 101, 103, 104
Purgold, Nikolai, 73–74
Purgold, Vladimir, 73–74, 99
Pushkin, Alexander, 26, 42, 75, 78, 88–90, 93, 98, 103, 124, 160

Ravelli, 164, 165
Repin, Elya, 114, 116, 117, 119–120, 128, 174–175
Rimsky-Korsakov, Nikolai, 57–59, 68, 72, 81, 84, 86, 87, 94, 97, 100, 101, 103, 109, 110, 138, 153, 156, 157, 159, 167, 170, 173, 175, 176
Rimsky-Korsakov, Voin, 102, 139
Rubinstein, Anton, 46–48, 56, 86, 94–96, 134, 162, 167

Schubert, Franz, 22, 150, 167
Serov, Alexander, 24, 25, 67
Shakespeare, William, 24, 26
Shestakova, Ludmilla, 68, 76, 77, 83, 88–90, 94, 113, 155, 157, 158, 167
Shilovsky, Stepan, 37–39, 44, 83
Shilovskaya, Maria, 37–39, 44, 83
Schumann, Robert, 22
Shostakovich, Dmitri, 139

Smetana, Bedrich, 71
Solomon, Henrietta Nissen, 47, 73
Sophocles, 43
Spinoza, Baruch, 114
Stassov, Dmitri, 148
Stassov, Vladimir, 24–26, 28, 29, 38, 39, 41, 47, 48, 50, 53, 60, 67, 69, 76, 77, 87, 89, 94, 97, 103, 110, 111, 113–117, 121–128, 130, 132, 133, 137, 140–142, 148–151, 153, 155, 157–160, 165, 167, 169, 172, 175, 176
Sutgov, General, 9

Tchaikovsky, Peter, 134–136
Tolstoy, Count Alexei, 161
Tolstoy, Lev (Leo), 24, 36, 50, 119, 120
Tretyakov, Pavel, 175
Turgenev, Ivan, 42, 136

Ulibishev, Alexander, 18–22, 49, 95

Vereshchagin, Vassily, 149

Wagner, Richard, 62, 94, 162
Wieniawsky, Henri, 47

Yegorova, Irina, 3

Zaremba, Nikolai, 56

DATE DUE

Reserve			
Sum 93			
O'Hagan			
GAYLORD			PRINTED IN U.S.A